Vocabulary WORKS

Level C

Joy Tweedt   Dr. Marjorie Merwin King   Dr. Alvin Granowsky

Copyright © 1995 by Modern Curriculum Press, Inc.

An imprint of Paramount Supplemental Education
250 James Street
Morristown, New Jersey 07960

All rights reserved. Manufactured in the United States of America. This book or parts thereof may not be reproduced in any form or mechanically stored in any retrieval system without written permission from the publisher. Published simultaneously in Canada by Globe/Modern Curriculum Press, Toronto.

ISBN 0-8136-1710-3

1 2 3 4 5 6 7 8 9 10   98 97 96 95 94

TABLE OF CONTENTS

ARTICLE	THEME	PAGE
Bee Bandits Busted	Nature	3
Sewing Is for the Birds!	Nature	8
Amazing Plant Comes Back to Life	Nature	13
On the Trail of a Kangaroo's Tail	Nature	18
Look at Those Dogs Go!	Entertainment	23
Dream World Explained!	Human Body	28
"Little House" Lady Lives on in Books	Heritage	33
Even the Moon Gets Blue	Language	38
Who Knows How Scratch-and-Sniff Stickers Are Made?	Technology	43
Small Wonders Score Big	Entertainment	48
Mysterious Goose Bumps Appear	Human Body	53
Widow Goes on Blind Date	Nature	58
This Gorilla Can Talk to You	Nature	63
Icebergs Lurk in Ocean	Nature	68
Who Is This Man on the Five Dollar Bill?	Heritage	73
Roadrunner Always on the Move	Nature	78
Killer Storm Hits!	Technology	83
Back to the Future	Heritage	88
Mind Boggling Movies	Entertainment	93
Young at Heart	Heritage	98
Glossary		103
Answer Key		108

BEE BANDITS BUSTED

The **robber** bees make their living by taking things that do not belong to them. They do not even make their own nests. They take them away from other bees. They rob others for food, too. It is **possible** for these bees to **force** other bees into doing what they want. Yet, these robber bees have no **stinger**. They use a kind of insect spray to get their way.

Here is how the thieves work. One or two of the thieves **enter** the nest they want to rob. There, they give off a spray that smells like lemons. Without a **battle**, the other bees leave their honey behind and rush away to the room where the baby bees are kept. A large number of thieves then **crowd** into the nest. They take wax and honey, which they **carry** to their own nest. The holdup may last **several** hours or even as long as a day or two. Finally, the **greedy** thieves leave and let the honey bees be.

"I THOUGHT THEY'D NEVER LEAVE!"
moans robber bee.

GETTING THE DETAILS

Which of these is <u>not</u> needed by the robber bees?
Check the best answer.

- [ ] wax
- [ ] a stinger
- [ ] honey
- [ ] a spray

ALPHABET GETS BUSY

Write the New Words in alphabetical order.

NEW WORDS
- robber
- several
- stinger
- carry
- crowd
- enter
- force
- battle
- possible
- greedy

1. _____
2. _____
3. _____
4. _____
5. _____
6. _____
7. _____
8. _____
9. _____
10. _____

WORDS MAKE MEANING

☞ **Context clues** are words in a sentence or phrase that help you understand the meaning of a word. Look for context clues in the story to help you match each New Word with its meaning. *Write the correct letter on each line.*

____ 1. greedy
____ 2. force
____ 3. battle
____ 4. enter
____ 5. robber
____ 6. crowd
____ 7. several
____ 8. possible
____ 9. carry
____ 10. stinger

a. a person who steals by using force or threats
b. a sharp, pointed part of an insect or animal
c. more than two but not many; a few
d. wanting or taking all that one can get with no thought of what others need; selfish
e. to come or go in or into
f. capable of existing or happening
g. to take from one place to another; to transport or conduct
h. any fight or struggle; conflict
i. to come together in a large group
j. to make or do something by using strength or power of some kind

SENTENCES LOSE STING WITHOUT WORDS

Finish these sentences. Write a New Word on each line.

1. Is it _____ for a bee to live without its _____?

2. The _____ was caught because he was _____ and came back for more.

3. Jim tried to _____ Kevin to _____ his books for him.

4. If it rains, the children will _____ the building and _____ together in the small hall.

5. _____ teams were in a _____ for first place.

ANTONYMS ARE OPPOSITE

Antonyms are words that have opposite meanings.

large and **small**

cold and **hot**

Write the antonym from the Word List in the correct box below.

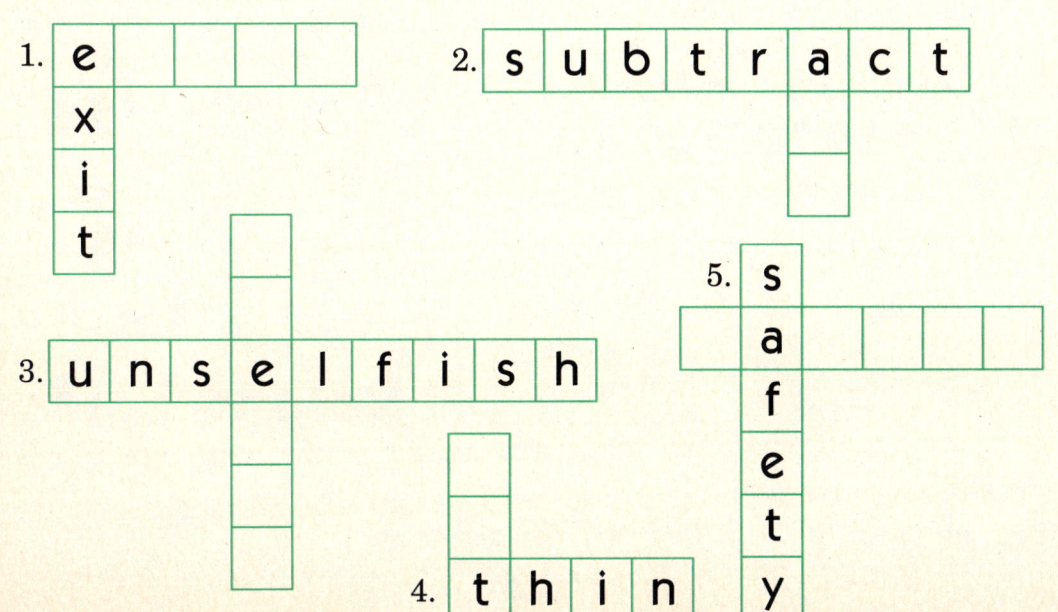

Word List
- danger
- enter
- teach
- fat
- add
- greedy

1. e _ _ _ _ (exit)
2. s u b t r a c t
3. u n s e l f i s h
4. t h i n y
5. s a f e t y
6. l e a r n

5

BOOK WRITERS BUMBLE, JUMBLE WORDS

Unscramble the New Words below.

1. grenist _____
2. deregy _____
3. wrodc _____
4. rente _____
5. salreve _____
6. borreb _____
7. rocfe _____
8. tatbel _____
9. boslespi _____
10. yracr _____

New Words
- battle
- carry
- greedy
- force
- stinger
- enter
- several
- crowd
- possible
- robber

ROBBER RAIDS HOME!
NEW WORDS USED TO TELL STORY

Imagine that you and a friend saw your dog running away with your neighbor's newspaper. Write a story with your friend telling about what happened.

The following questions will guide your writing.

- What would you do?
- How would you catch your dog?
- What would you say to your neighbor?

Use at least three New Words in your story.

READERS BUZZING ABOUT THESE GREAT BOOKS

READ:
- *Bees and Wasps* by Henry Pluckrose. (Gloucester Press, 1981)
- *The Bee* by Paul Starosta. (Charlesbridge, 1992)

BELIEVE ME

Bees cannot focus their eyes since they have no pupils.

Buzz over to the test!

TEST-TAKING SECRETS REVEALED

When you are asked to complete a sentence, read the entire sentence first. Then try each of the possible answers to see which one is best.

Read each sentence. Select the word that best completes the sentence. Fill in the circle for the answer at the bottom of the page.

1. You cannot _____ people to do what they do not want to do.
   - A   watch
   - B   force
   - C   crowd
   - D   invite

2. The _____ went into the store to take the owner's money.
   - A   robber
   - B   stinger
   - C   rubber
   - D   customer

3. You can _____ the cave through a small opening.
   - A   force
   - B   crowd
   - C   invite
   - D   enter

4. Awards were given to _____ police officers for their courage.
   - A   one
   - B   possible
   - C   several
   - D   no

5. The _____ of the bee has to be removed.
   - A   stingy
   - B   stinger
   - C   sting
   - D   stringy

6. Would you like a bag to _____ all your books?
   - A   carry
   - B   crowd
   - C   enter
   - D   force

Read each group of words. Select the answer that means the same as the underlined word. Fill in the circle for the answer at the bottom of the page.

7. <u>carry</u> the heavy load
   - A   unload
   - B   find
   - C   haul
   - D   weigh

8. a <u>greedy</u> giant
   - A   large
   - B   needy
   - C   quick
   - D   selfish

9. <u>possible</u> showers
   - A   likely
   - B   heavy
   - C   light
   - D   wet

10. for <u>several</u> days
    - A   no
    - B   a few
    - C   too many
    - D   many

11. <u>crowd</u> into a circle
    - A   run
    - B   join
    - C   space
    - D   squeeze

12. <u>battle</u> over the land
    - A   fight
    - B   plow
    - C   hurry
    - D   fly

ANSWERS

1 Ⓐ Ⓑ Ⓒ Ⓓ	4 Ⓐ Ⓑ Ⓒ Ⓓ	7 Ⓐ Ⓑ Ⓒ Ⓓ	10 Ⓐ Ⓑ Ⓒ Ⓓ
2 Ⓐ Ⓑ Ⓒ Ⓓ	5 Ⓐ Ⓑ Ⓒ Ⓓ	8 Ⓐ Ⓑ Ⓒ Ⓓ	11 Ⓐ Ⓑ Ⓒ Ⓓ
3 Ⓐ Ⓑ Ⓒ Ⓓ	6 Ⓐ Ⓑ Ⓒ Ⓓ	9 Ⓐ Ⓑ Ⓒ Ⓓ	12 Ⓐ Ⓑ Ⓒ Ⓓ

SEWING IS FOR THE BIRDS!
DAD MAKES NEST FOR BABY BIRDS

A **tailor** is a person who **sews** for a living. In southeast Asia, there is a bird that sews for its family. It is called a tailorbird. The **male** bird **prepares** a nest in which the **female** bird will lay her eggs. He finds two big leaves hanging close together on a tree and makes a nest out of them.

Here is how he does it. The tailorbird **pokes** holes in the leaves with his bill. Then he finds thread from a spider web or a plant. He **knots** the thread and puts it in and out of the holes, stitching the leaves together around the bottom. Next, he finds **material** to make the nest **fluffy** inside. At last, the nest is ready for the female. She will put her eggs in the tiny little nest. Soon after, her babies will be **hatched**.

KEYS TO STORY REVEALED

What does the tailorbird use to make holes in the leaves?

Check the best answer.

○ thread
○ his bill
○ fluffy material
○ a hatchet

Nature

ALPHABET ALL SEWED UP

Write the New Words in alphabetical order.

New Words

tailor　prepares
sews　material
male　fluffy
female　hatched
pokes　knots

1. _____
2. _____
3. _____
4. _____
5. _____
6. _____
7. _____
8. _____
9. _____
10. _____

WORDS HOLD NEST EGG OF MEANING

Match each New Word with its meaning. Write the correct letter on each line.

____ 1. fluffy

____ 2. pokes

____ 3. male

____ 4. hatched

____ 5. material

____ 6. knots

____ 7. prepares

____ 8. sews

____ 9. tailor

____ 10. female

a. of or for women or girls; of the group that is the mother of the offspring

b. makes ready

c. soft and light

d. fastens or joins with stitches

e. cloth or other fabric

f. to have brought forth young birds, fish, or turtles from eggs

g. fastenings made by tying together parts or pieces of such things as string and rope

h. a person who makes or repairs clothing

i. of or for men or boys; of the group that is the father of the offspring

j. pushes or jabs, as with a stick or finger

SENTENCE HOLES FILLED WITH WORDS

Finish these sentences. Write a New Word on each line.

New Words

1. My mother _____ clothes for all of us.
2. She bought some flowered _____ to make a new dress.
3. The _____ put new buttons on the suit.
4. He tied _____ in the thread so the buttons would stay in place.
5. Sally _____ the needle in and out of the fabric.
6. The _____ feathers were very soft.
7. Dad always _____ a delicious dinner.
8. The bird's eggs _____ yesterday.
9. Most _____ birds are brightly colored so they will attract a female.
10. The _____ birds have dull colors so they can hide in the nest.

tailor
sews
male
female
pokes
prepares
material
fluffy
hatched
knots

SO WHAT DO YOU SEW?

☞ **Homonyms** are words that sound alike but have different meanings and spellings.

know and **no**
so and **sew**

Need Help? Check out the glossary on page 103.

Draw lines to match the homonyms below.

1. creak   a. hair
2. or   b. oar
3. hare   c. creek

4. break   a. heal
5. male   b. brake
6. heel   c. mail

Choose the correct homonyms from the list at the left to complete these sentences.

a. We could have soup _____ a sandwich for lunch.
b. There is a small bridge over the _____ .
c. You should comb your _____ for the picture.
d. The _____ of Mary's shoe is worn down.
e. Most _____ birds do not sit on the eggs.

THE WORD SEARCH IS ON

Find the New Words and circle them.

```
F Q K N O T S C M R
E T A I L O R V A H
M A L E Y S W A T L
A M K Z O E P P E X
L B E D J W O V R M
E K H I E S K C I D
P R E P A R E S A W
P R Q A D C S Y L T
L N F L U F F Y E C
R D H A T C H E D L
```

Royal Tailors Create Togs For Top Dogs

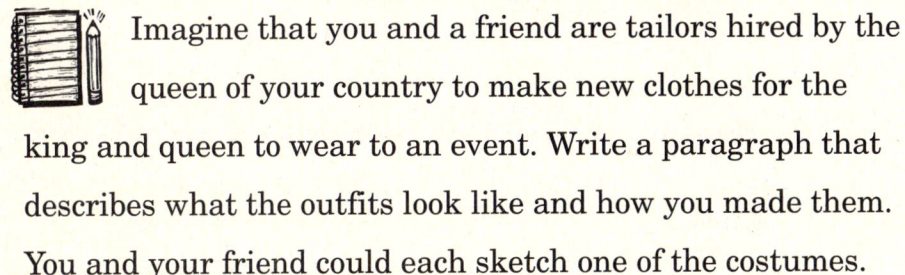

Imagine that you and a friend are tailors hired by the queen of your country to make new clothes for the king and queen to wear to an event. Write a paragraph that describes what the outfits look like and how you made them. You and your friend could each sketch one of the costumes.

The following questions will help you get started.
- What materials did you use?
- What does the clothing look like?
- What is the special occasion to be?

Use at least three New Words in your sentences.

BUILD YOUR OWN NEST EGG WITH THESE INTERESTING BOOKS AND MAGAZINES

- *Animals of South East Asia* by Margaret Ayer. (St. Martins Press, 1970)
- *Science World Magazine.* (Feb. 11, 1994)

THESE FACTS ARE FOR THE BIRDS

- The character Darzie in *Jungle Book* by Rudyard Kipling is actually a tailorbird.

- The nest of the hummingbird is only an inch wide or about the size of a nut.

- The yellow warbler doesn't build a nest. It lays its eggs in other birds' nests.

Fly over to the test!

SCORE HIGHER ON TESTS

Decide the meaning of underlined words before you look at the answer choices.

Read each group of words. Select the answer that means the same as the underlined word. Fill in the circle for the answer at the bottom of the page.

1. a male child
   - A strong
   - B wild
   - C boy
   - D tame

2. sews his clothes
   - A reads
   - B stitches
   - C washes
   - D irons

3. pokes a hole in
   - A scratches
   - B jabs
   - C rubs
   - D burns

4. a fluffy cloud
   - A dark
   - B large
   - C soft
   - D white

5. a female student
   - A scary
   - B girl
   - C common
   - D boy

6. prepares for school
   - A gets ready
   - B leaves
   - C hurries off
   - D starts

Read each set of sentences. Select the word that best completes the second sentence in the set. Fill in the circle for the answer at the bottom of the page.

7. Jeff used the material to make a costume for the play. Material means—
   - A cloth
   - B paper
   - C thread
   - D mask

8. Lynn tied knots in the rope to keep it from slipping. Knots are—
   - A ribbons
   - B strands
   - C buttons
   - D fastenings

9. The tailor fixed the suit so that it would fit. A tailor is someone who—
   - A irons
   - B sews
   - C presses
   - D buys

10. The birds hatched from their eggs in late spring. Hatched means—
    - A shaded
    - B ate
    - C came out
    - D made

11. The tailorbird sews the leaves together to make a nest. Sews means—
    - A stacks
    - B fastens
    - C presses
    - D plants

12. When he wants my attention, he pokes me in the arm. Pokes means—
    - A brushes
    - B scrapes
    - C pushes
    - D forces

ANSWERS

1 Ⓐ Ⓑ Ⓒ Ⓓ	4 Ⓐ Ⓑ Ⓒ Ⓓ	7 Ⓐ Ⓑ Ⓒ Ⓓ	10 Ⓐ Ⓑ Ⓒ Ⓓ
2 Ⓐ Ⓑ Ⓒ Ⓓ	5 Ⓐ Ⓑ Ⓒ Ⓓ	8 Ⓐ Ⓑ Ⓒ Ⓓ	11 Ⓐ Ⓑ Ⓒ Ⓓ
3 Ⓐ Ⓑ Ⓒ Ⓓ	6 Ⓐ Ⓑ Ⓒ Ⓓ	9 Ⓐ Ⓑ Ⓒ Ⓓ	12 Ⓐ Ⓑ Ⓒ Ⓓ

AMAZING PLANT COMES BACK TO LIFE

The resurrection (rez uh REK shuhn) plant is really **amazing**. It can dry up, blow away, and then come back to life. Its name even means "to come back from the dead." This plant is one of the few that can **wander** from place to place.

The resurrection plant lives in the **desert**. Since it hardly ever rains there, water is very **scarce**. When there is too little **moisture**, the plant dries up. Its roots come out of the ground. The whole plant is a ball of **twigs** that looks dead. As it **drifts**, it can **search** for water. When it finds enough moisture, the **roots** sink back into the ground. What seemed to be a dead plant returns to life. A **sprout** appears and the plant grows again.

When the ground becomes dry again, the plant will pull up its roots and move on. Once again, it will wander across the desert to look for water. Then it can come back to life and bloom again.

Details Take Root In Story

What does the resurrection plant do when it finds water?

Check the best answer.

○ Its roots come out of the ground.

○ It wanders around the desert.

○ It dies and becomes dried twigs.

○ Its roots grow into the ground.

Nature 13

ALPHABET BRANCHES OUT

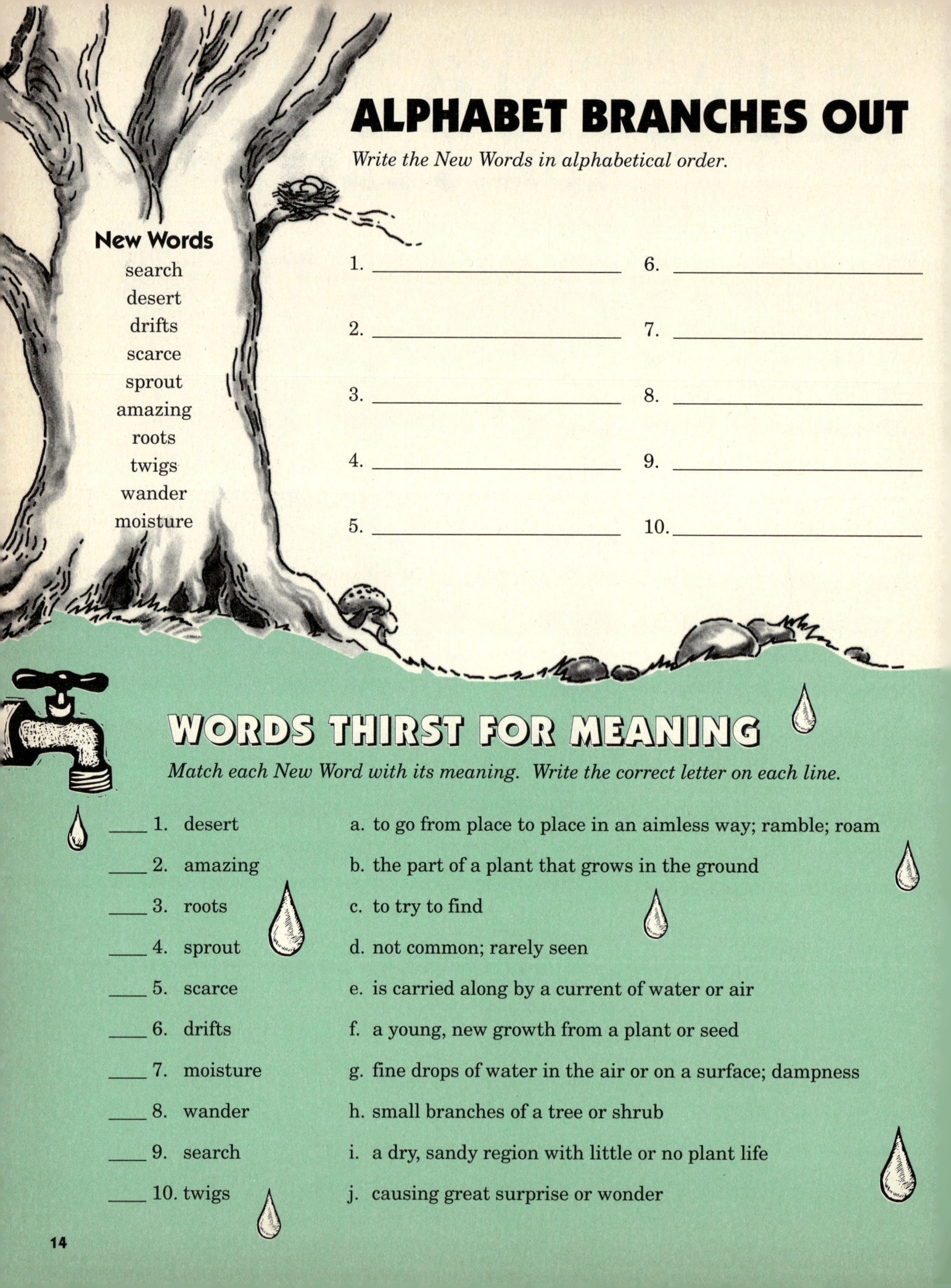

Write the New Words in alphabetical order.

New Words

search
desert
drifts
scarce
sprout
amazing
roots
twigs
wander
moisture

1. _____ 6. _____
2. _____ 7. _____
3. _____ 8. _____
4. _____ 9. _____
5. _____ 10. _____

WORDS THIRST FOR MEANING

Match each New Word with its meaning. Write the correct letter on each line.

___ 1. desert
___ 2. amazing
___ 3. roots
___ 4. sprout
___ 5. scarce
___ 6. drifts
___ 7. moisture
___ 8. wander
___ 9. search
___ 10. twigs

a. to go from place to place in an aimless way; ramble; roam
b. the part of a plant that grows in the ground
c. to try to find
d. not common; rarely seen
e. is carried along by a current of water or air
f. a young, new growth from a plant or seed
g. fine drops of water in the air or on a surface; dampness
h. small branches of a tree or shrub
i. a dry, sandy region with little or no plant life
j. causing great surprise or wonder

SENTENCES SPROUT NEW WORDS

Finish these sentences. Write a New Word on each line.

1. The strong wind blew some _____ off the tree.
2. We decided to _____ through the carnival.
3. Carrots are really the _____ of the plant.
4. We watched the magician perform _____ tricks with a rope.
5. The snow _____ over the roads and sidewalks.
6. A deer had nibbled the tender _____ of the plant.
7. The rain brought a little _____ to the dry areas.
8. Carlos will _____ for his missing notebook.
9. Water is _____ in the desert.
10. The cactus is a plant that lives in the _____.

WORDS HAVE HAPPY ENDINGS

☞ **Endings** can be added to many words. Sometimes the spelling of a word must be changed when an ending is added.

Ending Rules

Add s to form the plural of most words.
book + s = books

Add es to form the plural of a word that ends in ch, sh, s, or x.
punch + es = punches

If a word ends in a consonant and y, change the y to an i when adding the ending es or ed.
copy + ed = copied

If a word with a short vowel ends in a single consonant, double the final consonant before adding ed or ing.
drop + ing = dropping

If a word ends in e, drop the e before adding ed or ing.
wipe + ing = wiping

Add the endings shown to the words listed below. Check the ending rules to see if spelling changes are needed.

WORD	S or ES	ED	ING
1. search			
2. carry			
3. hope			
4. drip			

ANALOGIES ARE EVERYWHERE

Analogies show the relationships between things.

book is to **read** as **song** is to **sing**

finger is to **hand** as **toe** is to **foot**

Complete the following analogies using the words listed in the box below.

Word List
moisture
scarce
amazing
search
roots
desert

1. sand is to _____ as ice is to glacier
2. _____ is to plentiful as few is to many
3. _____ is to surprising as sharp is to pointed
4. _____ is to soil as branches is to air
5. electricity is to lightning as _____ is to cloud
6. _____ is to discover as seek is to find

GROWTHS APPEAR IN BACKYARD

Write three sentences comparing the tree and the cactus.

The following questions will help guide you in writing your sentences.
- What is alike about the tree and the cactus?
- What is different?
- What do both need in order to grow?

Use at least three New Words in your sentences.

Read More About Amazing Plants

- *Don't Tickle the Elephant Tree* by Philip Barnard. (Julian Messner, 1982)
- *Eyewitness: Plants* by David Burnie. (Knopf, 1989)
- *Seeds to Plants* by Jeffery Bates. (Gloucester Press, 1991)

BUILT IN WATER COOLER STOPS THIRST

The largest cactus in the world, the saguaro, can hold almost ten tons of water. It stores the water for use during the dry months.

Drift on over to the test.

TEST-DAY TIPS TOLD

When looking for a word that means the opposite of another word, don't be fooled by a choice that means the same.

Read each phrase. Select the answer that means the opposite of the underlined word. Fill in the circle for the answer at the bottom of the page.

1. a sprout appears
   - A fly
   - B new shoot
   - C old branch
   - D plant

2. felt the moisture
   - A wetness
   - B dryness
   - C softness
   - D hardness

3. a scarce jewel
   - A common
   - B uncommon
   - C beautiful
   - D expensive

4. an amazing animal
   - A wonderful
   - B unusual
   - C fast
   - D ordinary

5. wander for awhile
   - A drive
   - B roam
   - C walk along
   - D stand still

Complete each definition with the best word. Fill in the circle for the answer at the bottom of the page.

6. Small branches on a tree are called . . . .
   - A roots
   - B trunks
   - C twigs
   - D leaves

7. To explore for something is to . . . .
   - A sprout
   - B search
   - C drift
   - D call

8. Land with very little rainfall is a . . . .
   - A moisture
   - B rain forest
   - C desert
   - D island

9. When an object is carried by the wind, it . . . .
   - A searches
   - B roots
   - C sprouts
   - D drifts

10. The parts of a plant that hold it to the ground are called . . . .
    - A twigs
    - B roots
    - C weeds
    - D branches

11. To be rare and hard to find is to be . . . .
    - A amazing
    - B lost
    - C scarce
    - D ugly

12. To roam or move around is to . . . .
    - A wave
    - B fly
    - C wonder
    - D wander

ON THE TRAIL OF A KANGAROO'S TAIL

You may know that **kangaroos** carry their babies in a **pouch**. But did you know that kangaroos carry a chair and a **crutch**, too? The chair and the crutch are really their tails.

The kangaroo's tail is very **powerful**. A kangaroo never has to look for a seat. It just sits down. Its strong tail becomes its chair. Its tail also helps it **travel** from place to place. To walk, the kangaroo puts down its front paws. It puts its tail under its heavy body. It uses its tail like a crutch. The tail holds up the whole back part of the body as the back legs swing **forward**.

To go fast, a kangaroo jumps. It can **leap** across a classroom or even over an **automobile** in one jump. It is also very fast. It uses its tail to keep its **balance** as it speeds along.

Next time you want to tell a story, why not tell the amazing **tale** of the kangaroo's tail?

STORY HOPPING WITH DETAILS

What is one thing that a kangaroo can jump over?

Check the best answer.

❑ a school building ❑ a car
❑ a mountain ❑ a circus tent

18 Nature

ALPHABET KEEPS LETTERS IN ORDER

Write the New Words in alphabetical order.

New Words
- leap
- balance
- pouch
- kangaroos
- automobile
- crutch
- powerful
- travel
- forward
- tale

1. _____
2. _____
3. _____
4. _____
5. _____
6. _____
7. _____
8. _____
9. _____
10. _____

WORDS AND MEANINGS — MATCH THEM UP

Match each New Word with its meaning. Write the correct letter on the line next to the word.

____ 1. kangaroos

____ 2. pouch

____ 3. crutch

____ 4. powerful

____ 5. forward

____ 6. leap

____ 7. balance

____ 8. tale

____ 9. automobile

____ 10. travel

a. anything that gives support or help; something that can be leaned on

b. toward a point in front

c. a story, especially about things that are imagined or made up

d. animals of Australia with short forelegs and strong, large hind legs, with which they make long leaps

e. a car; a vehicle moved by an engine that is part of it

f. to move oneself suddenly from the ground by using the leg muscles; jump; spring

g. to go from one place to another

h. having much power; strong or influential

i. a loose fold of skin, like a pocket, on the belly of certain female animals in which they carry their newborn young

j. the ability to keep one's body steady without falling; stability

19

SUFFIXES GET WORDS HOPPING

☞ A **root word** is a word or word part that is used as a base for making other words. A **suffix** is a word part that can be added to the end of a root word. Adding a suffix changes the meaning of the root word. The suffix **ful** means full of, or likely to.

Root word   Suffix   New word
hope   +   **ful**   =   **hopeful**

Finish the sentences by adding the suffix ful to the root word that is underlined.

1. If a machine is full of power, it is _____.
2. If you are full of joy, you are _____.
3. If you are full of thought, you are _____.
4. If a picture is full of color, it is _____.
5. If you are likely to forget, you are _____.
6. If you are full of care, you are _____.
7. If you are likely to help, you are _____.
8. If you are full of cheer, you are _____.

NEW WORDS COMPLETE SENTENCES

Finish these sentences. Write a New Word on each line.

1. The tow truck pulled the _____ from the ditch.
2. Its _____ engine roared as it pulled the heavy weight.
3. Jane wrote a _____ about a mouse from Mars.
4. In the story, the mouse decided to _____ to earth.
5. The _____ are my favorite animals to watch at the zoo.
6. Sometimes I can see a baby kangaroo peeking out of its mother's _____.
7. Rich has had to use a _____ since he broke his leg.
8. He had to learn how to move _____ using them.
9. Jenny kept her _____ while walking on the beam.
10. She can _____ off the beam and land perfectly.

New Words

kangaroos

forward

tale

pouch

automobile

powerful

crutch

travel

leap

balance

20

STRANGE DRAWINGS ARE BAFFLING

Write the New Word that matches each picture.

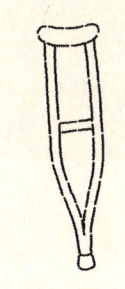

1. _____
2. _____
3. _____
4. _____

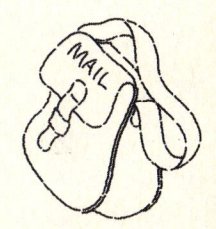

5. _____
6. _____
7. _____
8. _____

HOP OVER TO THE ZOO

Write a note to your parents trying to talk them into taking you to the zoo to see the kangaroos.

The following questions will help you in writing your note.

- Why do you want to see the kangaroos?
- What have you learned about kangaroos in school?
- Why should your parents take you to the zoo?

Use at least three New Words in your sentences.

Hop to the test!

JUMP INTO THESE BOOKS

- *Young Kangaroo* by Margaret Wise Brown. (Hyperion Books, 1993)
- *The Mother Kangaroo* by Edith Thacher Hurd. (Little, Brown, 1976)
- *Katy No Pocket* by Emmy Payne. (Houghton Mifflin, 1989)

THAT'S AMAZING!

A baby kangaroo, called a joey, is so small when it is born that it would fit in a teaspoon, with room to spare.

SECRETS TO SUCCESS ON TESTS

Look over the entire test before you begin. Make sure you understand what you will be doing.

Read each set of sentences. Select the answer that best completes the second sentence in the set. Fill in the circle for the answer at the bottom of the page.

1. We visited the <u>kangaroos</u> at the zoo. <u>Kangaroos</u> are animals that have—
   - A a mane
   - B two feet
   - C a pouch
   - D two tails

2. John needed a <u>crutch</u> to be able to walk. A <u>crutch</u> is a—
   - A vehicle
   - B support
   - C shoe
   - D chair

3. The kangaroo uses its <u>powerful</u> tail as a chair. <u>Powerful</u> means—
   - A strong
   - B large
   - C heavy
   - D thick

4. We parked the <u>automobile</u> in the garage. <u>Automobile</u> means—
   - A engine
   - B plane
   - C train
   - D car

5. The kangaroo carries its baby in its <u>pouch</u>. <u>Pouch</u> means—
   - A animal cage
   - B fold of skin
   - C purse
   - D tail

6. I am planning to <u>travel</u> to California this summer. <u>Travel</u> means—
   - A walk
   - B run
   - C go
   - D write

7. The tardy student told a <u>tale</u> that was hard to believe. <u>Tale</u> means—
   - A end
   - B story
   - C lie
   - D joke

8. The soldiers marched <u>forward</u> into battle. <u>Forward</u> means—
   - A back
   - B ahead
   - C over
   - D behind

Read each group of words. Select the answer that means the <u>same</u> as the underlined word. Fill in the circle for the answer at the bottom of the page.

9. will <u>leap</u> across
   - A jump
   - B swim
   - C walk
   - D ahead

10. <u>travel</u> to another city
    - A go
    - B come
    - C run
    - D plane

11. lost his <u>balance</u>
    - A lunch money
    - B stability
    - C way home
    - D support

12. stepped <u>forward</u>
    - A back
    - B ahead
    - C over
    - D behind

ANSWERS

1 Ⓐ Ⓑ Ⓒ Ⓓ	4 Ⓐ Ⓑ Ⓒ Ⓓ	7 Ⓐ Ⓑ Ⓒ Ⓓ	10 Ⓐ Ⓑ Ⓒ Ⓓ
2 Ⓐ Ⓑ Ⓒ Ⓓ	5 Ⓐ Ⓑ Ⓒ Ⓓ	8 Ⓐ Ⓑ Ⓒ Ⓓ	11 Ⓐ Ⓑ Ⓒ Ⓓ
3 Ⓐ Ⓑ Ⓒ Ⓓ	6 Ⓐ Ⓑ Ⓒ Ⓓ	9 Ⓐ Ⓑ Ⓒ Ⓓ	12 Ⓐ Ⓑ Ⓒ Ⓓ

LOOK AT THOSE DOGS GO! HUSKIES HOOF IN A HURRY

Can you guess what the state **sport** of Alaska is? It's not skiing. It's not skating. It's sled dog **racing**! Every March the Iditarod Trail Sled Dog Race is held. For over ten days, people called **mushers** race their dogs about 1,200 miles, from Anchorage to Nome.

Siberian **huskies** are used as sled dogs. Sled dogs must work as a team to pull the musher, who stands on the back of the sled.

Mushers have no **reins** to hold, so they use their **voices** to steer their teams. They have a special **language**. A musher calls "Hike!" to start the team. "Gee!" means turn right, "Haw!" means go left, and "Whoa!" means stop.

The race goes through Alaskan **wilderness**—mountains, frozen rivers, and forests. It can get as cold as 50 degrees below zero! The **courage** of the mushers is put to the test. They have to fight against the cold, deep snow, storms, lack of sleep, and **sometimes** even moose!

"I'll be dog gone!" exclaims one musher.

FIND THE DETAILS IN RECORD TIME

Where does the Iditarod end?

Check the best answer.

❑ Alaska

❑ Nome

❑ Anchorage

❑ Iditarod

Entertainment 23

ALPHABET KEPT IN ORDER

Write the New Words in alphabetical order.

1. _____
2. _____
3. _____
4. _____
5. _____

6. _____
7. _____
8. _____
9. _____
10. _____

New Words

sport
racing
mushers
wilderness
courage
sometimes
huskies
reins
voices
language

MATCH WORDS AND MEANINGS IN A HURRY

Match each New Word with its meaning.

Write the letter of the meaning on the line next to the word.

_____ 1. sport
_____ 2. racing
_____ 3. mushers
_____ 4. wilderness
_____ 5. courage
_____ 6. sometimes
_____ 7. huskies
_____ 8. reins
_____ 9. voices
_____ 10. language

a. a wild region or wasteland
b. bravery
c. the act of taking part in a contest of speed
d. sounds of people speaking
e. active play that is done to a set of rules
f. human speech or writing that stands for speech
g. once in a while
h. dog sled drivers
i. narrow strips of leather used to guide horses or dogs
j. strong dogs used for pulling sleds

WORDS RACE TO FINISH SENTENCES

Write the New Word that best completes each sentence.

1. It takes a lot of _____ to race the Iditarod.
2. Out in the _____ you are all by yourself.
3. The _____ load their sleds with food and warm clothing.
4. Sled dog racing is a _____ that is not for everybody.
5. _____ it gets very cold in Alaska.
6. The musher heard _____ as she got near the finish line.
7. There are no _____ on a dog sled.
8. Mushers have a special _____ that they use to speak to the dogs.
9. Sled dog _____ is a very popular sport in Alaska.
10. Mushers put booties on their _____ when the weather gets very cold.

WORD MEANINGS CHANGED

☞ A **prefix** is a word part that can be added to the beginning of a root word. Adding a prefix changes the meaning of the root word.

The prefix **un** means <u>not</u> or <u>opposite of</u>.

Add the prefix un to make a word that means the opposite of each underlined word.

Meaning

1. not <u>real</u>
2. opposite of <u>tie</u>
3. opposite of <u>wrap</u>
4. not <u>eaten</u>

New Word

1. _____
2. _____
3. _____
4. _____

Use the new words to complete these sentences.

5. Please _____ my shoelace.
6. Jim left the table with his supper _____ .
7. You should know that ghosts are _____ .
8. Janet will _____ her presents on her birthday.

SOLVE THIS PUZZLE AND WIN THE RACE

Use the New Words to complete the crossword puzzle.

ACROSS
3. sounds from the mouth
6. spoken or written words
7. straps used for controlling
10. sled dogs

DOWN
1. moving at great speed
2. area where nobody lives
4. at times
5. people who drive dog sleds
8. active game
9. fearlessness

New Words

sport
racing
mushers
wilderness
courage
sometimes
huskies
reins
voices
language

MY EXPERIENCES AS AN ALASKAN MUSHER

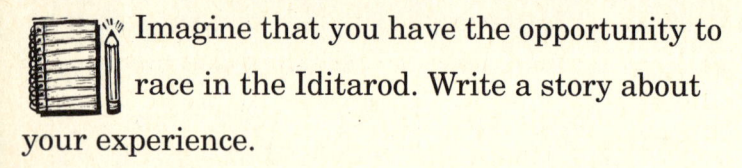

Imagine that you have the opportunity to race in the Iditarod. Write a story about your experience.

Use these questions to help you get started in your writing:

- What kinds of preparations will you make?
- How do you think you will feel out in the wilderness of Alaska all by yourself?
- What will you do when you reach the finish line?

Use at least three of the New Words in your story.

MUSHERS DON'T SAY "MUSH!"

The word *mush* probably comes from the French word *marchons*, which means "Let's go!" Today's racers never actually say "Mush," but they're still called mushers.

MORE ABOUT MUSHING!

READ:

- "Dog Race in Alaska." (*Boys' Life*, December, 1993)

- *Mush! Across Alaska in the World's Longest Sled-Dog Race* by Patricia Seibert. (Millbrook Press, 1992)

- "Ready, Set, Hike!" (*American Girl*, January/February, 1994)

Sled over to the test!

SECRETS TO SUCCESS ON TESTS

On test day, bring your own eraser and make sure it erases cleanly.

Read each group of words. Select the word or words that mean the <u>same</u> as the underlined word. Fill in the circle for the answer at the bottom of the page.

1 great <u>courage</u>
- **A** skill
- **B** desire
- **C** bravery
- **D** want

2 <u>language</u> class
- **A** history
- **B** speech and writing
- **C** geography
- **D** mathematics

3 heard <u>voices</u>
- **A** talking
- **B** fighting
- **C** noise
- **D** scratching

4 <u>huskies</u> pulled
- **A** people
- **B** horses
- **C** dogs
- **D** donkeys

5 through the <u>wilderness</u>
- **A** park
- **B** city
- **C** school yard
- **D** wild area

6 <u>mushers</u> called
- **A** drivers
- **B** dogs
- **C** cooks
- **D** teachers

7 played a <u>sport</u>
- **A** board game
- **B** game of cards
- **C** active game
- **D** musical instrument

8 <u>sometimes</u> want
- **A** now and then
- **B** often
- **C** seldom
- **D** all the time

Read each set of sentences. Select the word that completes the first sentence according to the stated meaning. Fill in the circle for the answer at the bottom of the page.

9 I ____ feel that I would like to be an astronaut. Which word indicates that the speaker feels this way once in a while?
- **A** always
- **B** never
- **C** sometimes
- **D** frequently

10 The boys enjoy ____ around the track. Which word indicates that what the boys enjoy is going very fast around the track?
- **A** being
- **B** jogging
- **C** walking
- **D** racing

11 He took the ____ in his hands to control the horse. Which word indicates he took narrow strips of leather attached to a bit?
- **A** rains
- **B** reins
- **C** mushers
- **D** wilderness

12 Do you enjoy the ____ of basketball? Which word indicates that basketball is an active game played to rules?
- **A** language
- **B** excitement
- **C** pace
- **D** sport

ANSWERS

1	Ⓐ Ⓑ Ⓒ Ⓓ	4	Ⓐ Ⓑ Ⓒ Ⓓ	7	Ⓐ Ⓑ Ⓒ Ⓓ	10	Ⓐ Ⓑ Ⓒ Ⓓ
2	Ⓐ Ⓑ Ⓒ Ⓓ	5	Ⓐ Ⓑ Ⓒ Ⓓ	8	Ⓐ Ⓑ Ⓒ Ⓓ	11	Ⓐ Ⓑ Ⓒ Ⓓ
3	Ⓐ Ⓑ Ⓒ Ⓓ	6	Ⓐ Ⓑ Ⓒ Ⓓ	9	Ⓐ Ⓑ Ⓒ Ⓓ	12	Ⓐ Ⓑ Ⓒ Ⓓ

DREAM WORLD EXPLAINED!
HUMAN BRAIN FOUND SLEEPING ON THE JOB

Dreams are like stories people watch in their sleep. But what is the truth about the strange world of dreams? People have **studied** dreams. Here is what they have found.

Everyone dreams. Most **adults** dream from three to five times in one night. Each dream lasts from ten to thirty minutes. People dream about things that have just happened. They dream about events they have thought about **recently**. They **hardly** ever dream about things that took place more than two days before.

Most people dream in color. People who have always been **blind**, however, do not see anything **during** their dreams. They dream of sounds, feelings, tastes, and smells.

People do not dream when they are in deep or **sound** sleep. They dream during times when they are nearly awake. Dreaming is helpful **though**. People who are not **allowed** to dream become very grouchy. People often say **grouchy** people "got up on the wrong side of the bed." Maybe they should say, "Go back and dream awhile!"

"Dreams are nonsense!" declares grouch.

What's the Big Idea?
What is the main idea of this story?
Check the best answer.
- ☐ People have studied dreams and found out many things.
- ☐ Most people dream in color.
- ☐ Dreams can come true.
- ☐ People who dream are never grouchy.

28 Human Body

VOCABULARY WISHES AND ALPHABET DREAMS

NEW WORDS

recently   blind
grouchy   sound
adults   allowed
though   studied
hardly   during

Write the New Words in alphabetical order.

1. _____
2. _____
3. _____
4. _____
5. _____
6. _____
7. _____
8. _____
9. _____
10. _____

Discover the hidden meaning
READ AGAIN!

Need help? Check out the glossary on page 103.

Match each New Word with its meaning. Write a letter on each line.

____ 1. studied   a. almost not; scarcely
____ 2. adults   b. let be done; permitted
____ 3. recently   c. deep and undisturbed
____ 4. hardly   d. looked at or into carefully; examined or investigated
____ 5. blind   e. throughout the whole time of; all through
____ 6. during   f. men or women who are fully grown up; mature people
____ 7. though   g. to be in a bad mood; cross and complaining
____ 8. allowed   h. not able to see; having no sight
____ 9. grouchy   i. of a time just before now; lately
____ 10. sound   j. in spite of the fact that; although; however

DID YOU KNOW?

Animals have dreams and nightmares just like people do.

DREAM WORDS FIT PERFECTLY!

Finish these sentences. Write a New Word on each line.

NEW WORDS
blind
grouchy
sound
allowed
adults
hardly
during
though
recently
studied

1. Ben _____ the directions that came with the model.
2. He could not fit all the parts together, _____.
3. The _____ ate at a large table in the dining room.
4. But the children were _____ to eat outside at the picnic table.
5. Many _____ people develop an unusually good sense of hearing.
6. They respond to noise even when they are _____ asleep.
7. Mrs. Jackson _____ ever smiles.
8. She is always _____ no matter what happens.
9. My sister _____ won first place in a gymnastics contest.
10. I held my breath _____ her whole performance.

SUFFIXES PROVIDE HAPPY ENDINGS!

👉 A suffix is a word part that can be added to the end of a root word.

root word   suffix   new word

hard   +   ly   =   hardly

Add the suffix ly to each underlined word. Write the word in the box.

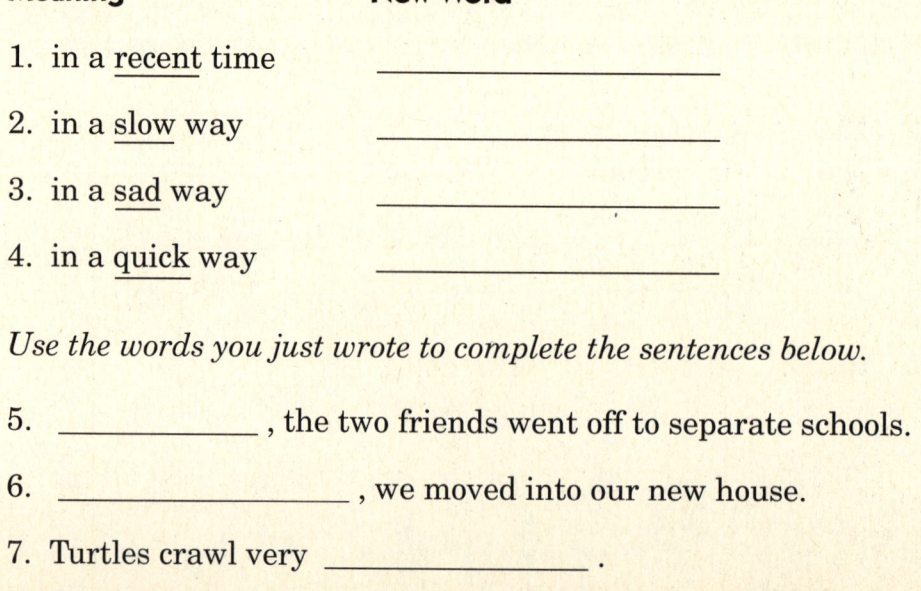

Meaning   **New Word**

1. in a <u>recent</u> time   _____
2. in a <u>slow</u> way   _____
3. in a <u>sad</u> way   _____
4. in a <u>quick</u> way   _____

Use the words you just wrote to complete the sentences below.

5. _____ , the two friends went off to separate schools.
6. _____ , we moved into our new house.
7. Turtles crawl very _____ .
8. The runners finished the race very _____ .

Bears sleep soundly two months yearly!

Be the Life of the Party!

Watch:
The Wizard of Oz, starring Judy Garland.

Read:
Amanda Dreaming, by Barbara Wersha. (Atheneum, 1973)

Dinosaur Dreams, by Allan Ahlberg. (Greenwillow Books, 1991)

The Wizard of Oz by L. Frank Baum. (Golden Press, 1986)

WORDS RIDDLED WITH SECRET MEANING!

Write the New Words in the blanks next to their clues. The answer to the riddle will appear in the shaded column.

Riddle: This dream is frightening and may cause you to wake up.

Clues

1. deep __ __ __ __ __
2. having no sight __ __ __ __ __
3. in a bad mood __ __ __ __ __ __ __
4. however __ __ __ __ __ __
5. looked at carefully __ __ __ __ __ __ __
6. do while sleeping d r e a m
7. grown-ups __ __ __ __ __ __
8. all through __ __ __ __ __ __ __
9. a short time ago __ __ __ __ __ __

Dream Child Tells All!

Do you remember your dreams? Do you dream in black and white or color? On another sheet of paper, write a short paragraph about a dream you have had. As you write, think about questions like these:

- Who was in your dream?
- What happened?
- How did your dream make you feel?

Use at least three of your New Words in your paragraph.

IMPROVE YOUR SCORE

If you skip a question in the test, be sure to skip the correct line in the answer box.

Read each group of words. Select the answer that means the same as the underlined word. Fill in the circle for the answer at the bottom of the page.

1 is helpful though
   - A maybe
   - B however
   - C also
   - D sometimes

2 heard it recently
   - A clearly
   - B purposely
   - C hardly
   - D lately

3 had a sound sleep
   - A deep
   - B restless
   - C noisy
   - D long

4 studied the problem
   - A caused
   - B dreamed
   - C looked at closely
   - D disagreed with

5 during the storm
   - A before
   - B at the time of
   - C after
   - D in between

6 hardly had time
   - A usually
   - B scarcely
   - C never
   - D easily

Read each sentence. Select the answer that best completes the sentence. Fill in the circle for the answer at the bottom of the page.

7 The ____ person has a seeing-eye dog.
   - A grouchy
   - B old
   - C sleeping
   - D blind

8 Both the children and the ____ enjoyed the clowns at the circus.
   - A adults
   - B people
   - C dreamers
   - D animals

9 I was not ____ to attend the game.
   - A sound
   - B studied
   - C dreamed
   - D allowed

10 She felt ____ because she was tired.
   - A studied
   - B grouchy
   - C blind
   - D sound

11 The alarm awoke me from a ____ sleep.
   - A blind
   - B grouchy
   - C sound
   - D allowed

12 I ____ ever watch sports on TV.
   - A hardly
   - B though
   - C during
   - D recently

"LITTLE HOUSE" LADY LIVES ON IN BOOKS

As a young girl, Laura Ingalls led an **interesting** life. She was **born** about one hundred thirty years ago in a little log **cabin** in the big north woods. She traveled west with her mother and father and her sister Mary in a covered wagon. They moved to Kansas and lived in a little house on the **prairie**. They moved to new **territory** that had just opened up to **settlers**.

When Laura Ingalls Wilder grew up, she married Almanzo Wilder. She wrote many books about her family's adventures. Her books are like time machines. They take your **mind** through time and **space** into the **past**. They help us see how people lived long ago. Some of her stories were made into a **television** show called *Little House on the Prairie*.

Laura Ingalls Wilder wrote ten books. In time, you may want to read them all. Then you can travel in time with Laura Ingalls Wilder, too.

A WALK DOWN MAIN-IDEA STREET

What is this story mainly about?
Check the best answer.

○ a little house on the prairie
○ a covered wagon that went to Kansas
○ a time machine
○ a lady who wrote about her life

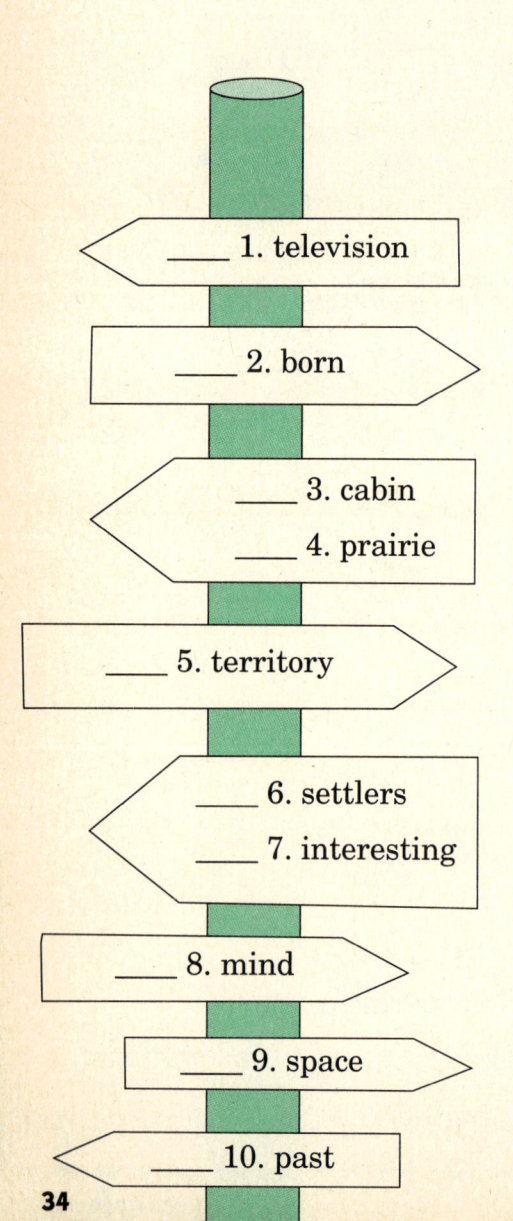

ALPHABET HELPS TELL STORIES

Write the New Words in alphabetical order.

NEW WORDS

cabin   television
prairie   settlers
interesting   space
past   born
mind   territory

1. _____   6. _____
2. _____   7. _____
3. _____   8. _____
4. _____   9. _____
5. _____   10. _____

WORDS FIND MISSING MEANINGS

Match each New Word with its meaning. Write the letter on the line next to the word.

____ 1. television
____ 2. born
____ 3. cabin
____ 4. prairie
____ 5. territory
____ 6. settlers
____ 7. interesting
____ 8. mind
____ 9. space
____ 10. past

a. an area of land ruled by a nation or state

b. stirring up one's interest; exciting

c. brought into life or being

d. the means of sending images by radio waves or wire to a receiver in another location; of, using, used in, or sent by television

e. the area that stretches in all directions, has no limits, and contains all things in the universe

f. the part of a person that thinks, reasons, feels, decides

g. the time that has gone by

h. people who go to live in a new country, colony, or region

i. a small house built in a simple, rough way, usually of wood

j. a large area of level or rolling, grassy land without many trees

Need Help? Check out the glossary on page 103.

SYLLABLES MAKE WORDS GROW

☞ Words can be divided into smaller word parts called **syllables**. For example, say the word radio and listen for its syllables.

ra di o

Write each word leaving a space between syllables. Use a dictionary if you are not sure where to divide a word.

1. television _____

2. prairie _____

3. territory _____

4. adventure _____

5. cabin _____

6. interesting _____

7. settlers _____

8. automobile _____

9. material _____

10. entertainment _____

MISSING WORDS
GOOD MEDICINE FOR SENTENCES

Read the paragraph below. Write the New Words that best complete the sentences.

We can learn much by studying our country's _____. Early _____ had plenty of unexplored land from which to choose a place to live. Some built a very small _____ on the plains. It could be a lonely life because they had few close neighbors on the broad, treeless, grassy _____. Families had plenty of _____ to do their farming, though. There was no _____ for entertainment. A boy or girl could stretch his or her _____ by reading, talking, and playing games. Once a _____ became settled, it would become a state. This _____ way of life will never return. In fact, it was all over before any of us were _____.

Discover the wonder right in your own home. Read these interesting books!

- *Laura Ingalls Wilder* by Carol Greene. (Children's Press, 1990)
- *West From Home* by Laura Ingalls Wilder. (Harper & Row, 1976)

MIXED UP WORDS UNSCRAMBLED

NEW WORDS
- mind
- past
- prairie
- television
- territory
- cabin
- interesting
- born
- settlers
- space

Unscramble these New Words.

1. riorteryt _____
2. sletrest _____
3. robn _____
4. spat _____
5. eiriarp _____
6. dimn _____
7. pecas _____
8. vineosliet _____
9. bainc _____
10. grinetestin _____

POSTAL WORKERS TIRED AFTER BIRTHDAY BLITZ

When Laura Ingalls Wilder turned 84, she received over 900 birthday cards!

TRUE OR FALSE?

All the stories and events in the *Little House* books actually happened.

Answer: True

FACTS ABOUT DANIEL BOONE REVEALED

Who was Daniel Boone? Look up Daniel Boone in the encyclopedia or another book. Find some information about this famous explorer. Write a short report.

The following questions will help you get started.
- What things did Daniel Boone do well?
- What territory did Daniel Boone explore?
- What experiences did Daniel Boone have in Texas?

Use at least three New Words in your report.

Giddyup to the test!

TEST-TAKING SECRETS REVEALED

Answer all test questions you're sure of. Don't spend a lot of time on difficult questions. After you have gone through the test once, go back to the questions you skipped.

Read each group of words. Select the answer that means the <u>opposite</u> of the underlined word. Fill in the circle for the answer at the bottom of the page.

1 lived in the <u>past</u>

   A years ago   C future
   B last year   D yesterday

2 an <u>interesting</u> class

   A boring   C hard
   B exciting   D long

3 <u>born</u> in a cabin

   A brought up   C died
   B brought forth   D lived

4 founded by <u>settlers</u>

   A writers   C wanderers
   B pioneers   D builders

Read the paragraphs. Select the words that best fit in the blanks. Fill in the circles for the answers at the bottom of the page.

In the early days of our country, many brave men and women traveled across the land until they reached a new __5__. There, they did the hard work of __6__ on the __7__. One of the first jobs they did was to build a __8__.

5 A television
    B territory
    C cabin
    D space

6 A television
    B mind
    C settlers
    D past

7 A mind
    B prairie
    C space
    D cabin

8 A space
    B prairie
    C cabin
    D television

One of the most popular inventions of modern times is the __9__. It can take your __10__ into times before you were even __11__. It can carry you through time and __12__ into the future.

9 A cabin
    B prairie
    C space
    D television

10 A space
     B television
     C past
     D mind

11 A born
     B past
     C interesting
     D settlers

12 A cabin
     B settlers
     C prairie
     D space

ANSWERS							
1	Ⓐ Ⓑ Ⓒ Ⓓ	4	Ⓐ Ⓑ Ⓒ Ⓓ	7	Ⓐ Ⓑ Ⓒ Ⓓ	10	Ⓐ Ⓑ Ⓒ Ⓓ
2	Ⓐ Ⓑ Ⓒ Ⓓ	5	Ⓐ Ⓑ Ⓒ Ⓓ	8	Ⓐ Ⓑ Ⓒ Ⓓ	11	Ⓐ Ⓑ Ⓒ Ⓓ
3	Ⓐ Ⓑ Ⓒ Ⓓ	6	Ⓐ Ⓑ Ⓒ Ⓓ	9	Ⓐ Ⓑ Ⓒ Ⓓ	12	Ⓐ Ⓑ Ⓒ Ⓓ

EVEN THE MOON GETS BLUE

People sometimes say that a thing happens "once in a blue moon." This means that it hardly ever happens. How did such a saying ever get started? The saying might have begun because there have been only a few times in **history** that the moon has ever really looked blue.

Over one hundred years ago, a **volcano** blew up. **Huge** rocks shot high into the air. Dust rose high into the **atmosphere**. Then the dust blew around the **globe**. The dust made the moon seem blue.

About seventy years later a huge **forest** fire happened in Canada. A great **amount** of smoke went into the atmosphere. People in that **area** saw a blue moon. **Disasters** that make the moon look blue do not happen often.

If someone says she only goes fishing "once in a blue moon," do not **expect** to see her out digging for worms any time soon.

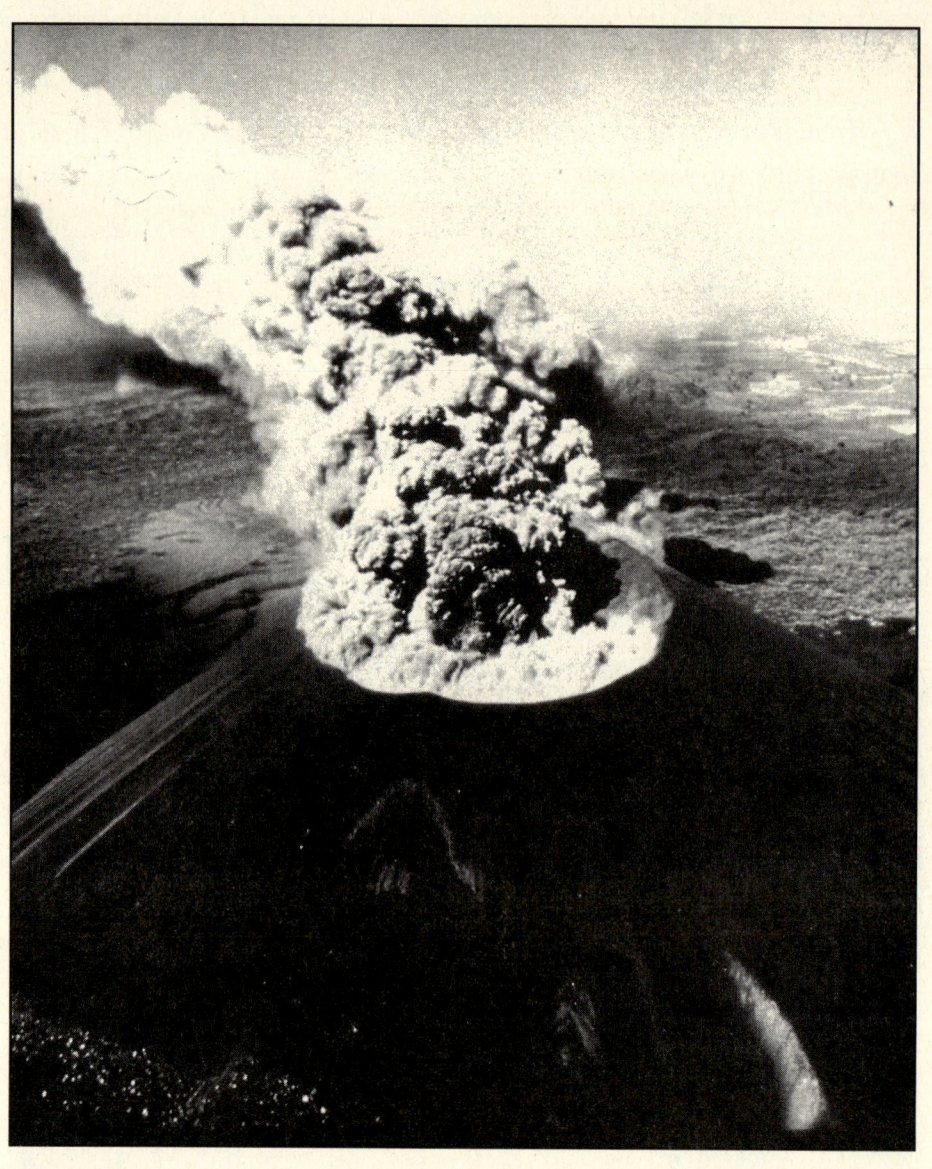

Dust from volcanoes can make the moon seem blue.

Main Idea Found Once in a Blue Moon

What is this story mainly about?

Check the best answer.

○ how people can make the moon look blue

○ why the moon should have been blue

○ what happens when a volcano blows up

○ how an old saying about the moon may have begun

38 Language

ALPHABET KEEPS WORDS IN ORDER

New Words

volcano
globe
expect
forest
history
amount
atmosphere
disasters
huge
area

Write the New Words in alphabetical order.

1. _____
2. _____
3. _____
4. _____
5. _____
6. _____
7. _____
8. _____
9. _____
10. _____

WORDS TAKE OFF IN SEARCH FOR MEANING

Match the New Words to their meanings. Write the correct letter on the line.

____ 1. history

____ 2. huge

____ 3. volcano

____ 4. atmosphere

____ 5. globe

____ 6. forest

____ 7. amount

____ 8. area

____ 9. disasters

____ 10. expect

a. very large; immense

b. the air around the earth

c. to think that something will happen or come; look forward to

d. all the recorded events of the past

e. the earth

f. a quantity

g. an opening in the earth's surface through which molten rock is thrown up

h. happenings that cause damage or suffering, as a flood or earthquake

i. a part of the earth's surface; region

j. a thick growth of trees covering a large piece of land; large woods

INCOMPLETE SENTENCES NEED HELP NOW!

Finish each sentence using a New Word.

New Words

- atmosphere
- forest
- globe
- expect
- huge
- disasters
- history
- volcano
- area
- amount

1. An elephant is certainly a _____ animal.
2. It can pull up trees from the _____ and carry them in its trunk.
3. That nearby mountain is actually a _____ .
4. People say that it has a _____ of erupting every 200 years.
5. The fire gave off a great _____ of black smoke.
6. A large _____ of the town turned dark.
7. If the earth's _____ were damaged, everything would change.
8. The land might get colder all over the _____ .
9. People did not _____ the earthquake to be so damaging.
10. _____ like these force many people from their homes.

SYNONYMS SEEM SIMILAR

☞ **Synonyms** are words with nearly the same meaning.

begin and **start**

pick and **choose**

Write the synonym next to each word.

Word List

- tale
- automobile
- large
- giggle
- quantity
- forest
- right
- dampness

Word	Synonym
1. huge	_____
2. chuckle	_____
3. amount	_____
4. moisture	_____
5. story	_____
6. woods	_____
7. car	_____
8. correct	_____

CLOSE STUDY REVEALS NEW WORDS

Find the hidden New Words and circle them.

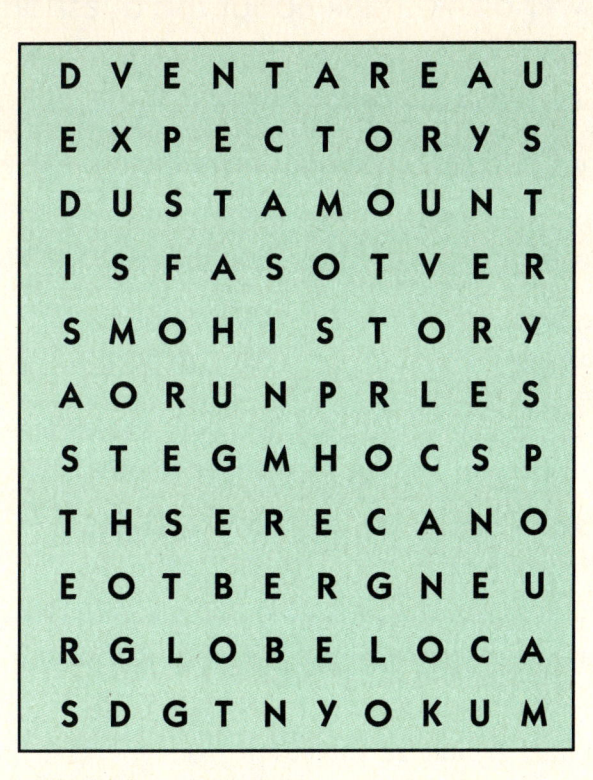

```
D V E N T A R E A U
E X P E C T O R Y S
D U S T A M O U N T
I S F A S O T V E R
S M O H I S T O R Y
A O R U N P R L E S
S T E G M H O C S P
T H S E R E C A N O
E O T B E R G N E U
R G L O B E L O C A
S D G T N Y O K U M
```

EXPRESS YOURSELF

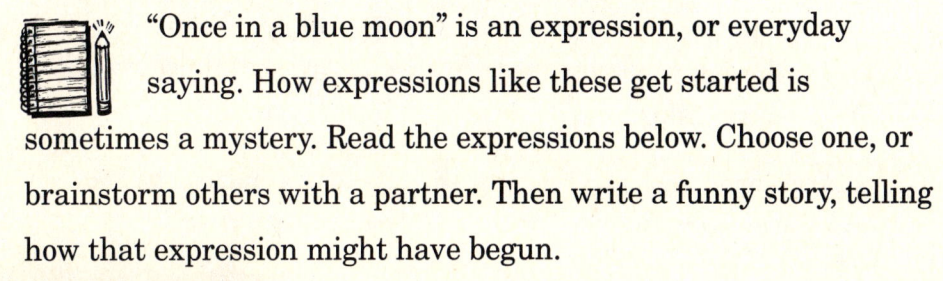

"Once in a blue moon" is an expression, or everyday saying. How expressions like these get started is sometimes a mystery. Read the expressions below. Choose one, or brainstorm others with a partner. Then write a funny story, telling how that expression might have begun.

It's raining cats and dogs.
He raced the clock.
Button your lip!
You're in the dog house.
Go jump in the lake!

The following questions will guide you in writing your story.
- Where does the story take place?
- What happens?
- Who first says the expression?

When you are done, draw a picture to go with your story. Use at least three New Words in your story.

DO THE MOON WALK ON YOUR OWN

Read:
- *The Earth's Moon* by Isaac Asimov. (Gareth Stevens, 1988)
- *The Moon And It's Exploration* by Necia Apfel. (Watts, 1982)
- *The Moon* by David Darling. (Dillon Press, 1984)

SOMEWHERE OVER THE MOONBOW!

Just like the earth can have a rainbow, the moon can have a moonbow! When raindrops catch the reflection of a bright moon, the same colors of a rainbow can be seen— but only while looking at the moon at night.

DID YOU KNOW?

The moon has no air, and since air carries sound, it is totally silent.

Shoot for the moon when you take the test!

SCORE HIGHER ON TESTS

Never leave an answer blank. Think about the question and make your very best guess.

Read each sentence. Select the word that best completes the sentence. Fill in the circle for the answer at the bottom of the page.

1. It is wise to learn the lessons of _____.

   A disaster   C history
   B globe   D volcano

2. Air pollution can damage the earth's _____.

   A volcano   C area
   B globe   D atmosphere

3. Pat did not _____ this honor to be given to her.

   A expect   C export
   B expert   D excel

4. A _____ forest was cut down to build those homes.

   A amount   C huge
   B friendly   D area

Complete each definition with the best word or group of words. Fill in the circle for the answer at the bottom of the page.

5. A sphere that stands for the earth is a . . . .

   A forest
   B globe
   C ball
   D circle

6. The total number of something is the . . . .

   A area
   B history
   C amount
   D atmosphere

7. Terrible events that cause great loss or damage are . . . .

   A volcanoes
   B forests
   C history
   D disasters

8. A hole in the earth from which hot rocks come out is a . . . .

   A tornado
   B disaster
   C volcano
   D earthquake

9. A large area covered by trees and bushes is called a . . . .

   A forest
   B frost
   C foreman
   D floor

10. A region or part of the earth could be called an . . . .

    A atmosphere
    B air
    C amount
    D area

11. The air that surrounds the earth is called the . . . .

    A area
    B globe
    C atmosphere
    D huge

12. To look forward to something is to . . . .

    A expect it
    B deny it
    C refuse it
    D accept it

ANSWERS

1 Ⓐ Ⓑ Ⓒ Ⓓ	4 Ⓐ Ⓑ Ⓒ Ⓓ	7 Ⓐ Ⓑ Ⓒ Ⓓ	10 Ⓐ Ⓑ Ⓒ Ⓓ
2 Ⓐ Ⓑ Ⓒ Ⓓ	5 Ⓐ Ⓑ Ⓒ Ⓓ	8 Ⓐ Ⓑ Ⓒ Ⓓ	11 Ⓐ Ⓑ Ⓒ Ⓓ
3 Ⓐ Ⓑ Ⓒ Ⓓ	6 Ⓐ Ⓑ Ⓒ Ⓓ	9 Ⓐ Ⓑ Ⓒ Ⓓ	12 Ⓐ Ⓑ Ⓒ Ⓓ

WHO KNOWS HOW SCRATCH-AND-SNIFF STICKERS ARE MADE? WE TELL ALL!

You put them on your notebook and in your desk. They are scratch-and-sniff stickers. You can **scratch** them to get a special **scent.** You might scratch a picture of a strawberry to get a strawberry smell. But how do scratch-and-sniff stickers work?

Scratch-and-sniff stickers have **tiny capsules** that hold **perfumes.** When you scratch the sticker, the perfume capsules open, and you smell the scent. When you have scratched off all the perfume capsules, the sticker wears out.

Scratch-and-sniff stickers are sometimes used to sell perfumes in **magazines** and in **advertising** that is sent through the mail. Some people don't like these kinds of stickers because the perfume smell makes them **cough** and sneeze.

The Jorvik Viking Museum in England uses the scratch-and-sniff idea in a **surprising** way. The museum sells a postcard with a picture of a Viking food market. If you scratch the postcard, you can smell the food in the market. What a **modern** way to get a taste of the past.

LOOK FOR THE MAIN IDEA

What is this article mainly about?

Check the best answer.

❑ magazine advertising using scratch-and-sniff stickers

❑ the Jorvik Viking Museum

❑ the smells used in scratch-and-sniff stickers

❑ how scratch-and-sniff stickers work and are used

Entertainment 43

STICK TO THE ALPHABET

Add the New Words to the alphabetical list.

New Words

- modern
- scratch
- scent
- tiny
- capsules
- perfumes
- magazines
- advertising
- cough
- surprising

actor
_____
_____
cardinal
_____
dinner
_____
mainly
_____

_____
piece
_____
_____
school
_____
secret
_____
_____

SCRATCHERS ARE MATCHERS

Match each New Word with its meaning.

Write the letter of the meaning on the line next to the word.

_____ 1. modern   a. collections of writings that come out regularly

_____ 2. scratch   b. odor or aroma

_____ 3. scent   c. very small

_____ 4. tiny   d. shocking or amazing

_____ 5. capsules   e. to scrape or rub

_____ 6. perfumes   f. small containers

_____ 7. magazines   g. pleasant smells or fragrances

_____ 8. advertising   h. public announcement of goods for sale

_____ 9. cough   i. of the period in which you live

_____ 10. surprising   j. to force air out of the throat

SNIFF OUT THE MISSING WORDS

Write the New Word that best completes each sentence.

1. I tried on different _____ at the store.
2. According to the _____ , this is the best computer to buy.
3. My family ordered three _____ for our reading pleasure.
4. When my cat comes near, my throat tickles, and I begin to _____ .
5. As you _____ the sticker, you open the capsules of perfume.
6. Some parts of that computer are so _____ they are hard to see.
7. I woke up to the _____ of the roses outside my window.
8. The medicine comes in _____ or in tablets.
9. I was pleased to see how _____ my new school appeared to be.
10. It is _____ to me that you aren't interested in sports.

SMALL WORDS COMBINE FOR NEW MEANING

☞ A **compound word** is a word made up of two smaller words.

foot + ball = football

cup + cake = cupcake

Read each meaning below. Underline the two words that form a compound word. Then write the compound word on the line.

MEANING   **COMPOUND WORD**

1. the <u>time</u> of a <u>life</u> — lifetime
2. a house for a dog — _____
3. a fish shaped like a star — _____
4. a coat to wear in rain — _____
5. a brush used to paint — _____
6. corn that will pop — _____
7. a flake of snow — _____
8. the day of your birth — _____
9. a bird that is blue — _____
10. a burn from the sun — _____

STICK IS TO STICKER AS TICK IS TO TICKER

Analogies show the relationship between things.

nose is to **smell** as **eye** is to **see**

hot is to **cold** as **black** is to **white**

Complete these analogies using the words in the Word List.

1. today is to _____ as yesterday is to old
2. _____ is to leaves as winter is to snow
3. small is to _____ as big is to large
4. _____ is to compound as don't is to contraction
5. reading is to _____ as watching is to television
6. person is to _____ as animal is to beast

Word List

lifetime   human
autumn   magazines
modern   tiny

SUPER SNIFFERS

Dogs have ten square inches of smell cells. People have one square inch.

THE NOSE KNOWS

Scientists say the nose can smell about ten thousand different odors!

GOOD FRIENDS STICK TOGETHER

Imagine that you have bought a new kind of scratch-and-sniff sticker. Write a note to a friend telling this person why you think the sticker is so great. Draw a picture of the sticker at the top of the note to share it with your friend.

These questions will help you get started:
- What does the sticker look and smell like?
- Why do you think the sticker is so special?
- What are you going to do with the sticker?

Use at least three of the New Words in your note.

YOU'VE JUST SCRATCHED THE SURFACE!

FIND OUT MORE ABOUT SMELLS BY READING THESE BOOKS:

- *Smelling* by Henry Pluckrose. (Watts, 1986)
- *Smelling* by Kathie B. Smith and Victoria Crenson. (Troll Associates, 1987)
- *What Your Nose Knows!* by Jane B. Moncure. (Children's Press, 1982)

I can smell the test from here!

TEST-DAY TIPS TOLD

When looking for a word that means the same as another, don't be fooled by a choice that means the opposite.

Read each group of words. Select the word or words that mean the same as the underlined word. Fill in the circle for the answer at the bottom of the page.

1. tiny bubbles
   - A metal
   - B very large
   - C very small
   - D fragile

2. scent of pine
   - A shape
   - B looks
   - C group
   - D odor

3. capsules of dye
   - A small containers
   - B large factories
   - C boxes
   - D bottles

4. read magazines
   - A books
   - B stories
   - C weekly or monthly publication
   - D letters to a friend

5. cough and sneeze
   - A force air from the lungs
   - B shuffle the feet
   - C stumble
   - D laugh

6. surprising results
   - A expected
   - B harmful
   - C happy
   - D unexpected

7. read the advertising
   - A notices of money owed
   - B notices about goods
   - C articles
   - D stories

8. modern ways
   - A of past times
   - B funny
   - C shiny
   - D of present times

Read each set of sentences. Select the word that completes the first sentence according to the stated meaning. Fill in the circle for the answer at the bottom of the page.

9. Our school is in a ____ building.
   Which word indicates that the building is up-to-date?
   - A tiny   C surprising
   - B modern   D old

10. It is ____ to me that Jeff could get here.
    Which word indicates the speaker did not expect Jeff to come?
    - A advertising   C clear
    - B modern   D surprising

11. I like smelling the ____ in the store.
    Which word indicates that what is liked is sweet or flowery smells?
    - A scent   C perfumes
    - B capsules   D magazines

12. What do you use to ____ the sticker?
    Which word indicates that you are being asked about what you use to scrape the sticker?
    - A scrap   C scrawl
    - B scratch   D screw

ANSWERS							
1	Ⓐ Ⓑ Ⓒ Ⓓ	4	Ⓐ Ⓑ Ⓒ Ⓓ	7	Ⓐ Ⓑ Ⓒ Ⓓ	10	Ⓐ Ⓑ Ⓒ Ⓓ
2	Ⓐ Ⓑ Ⓒ Ⓓ	5	Ⓐ Ⓑ Ⓒ Ⓓ	8	Ⓐ Ⓑ Ⓒ Ⓓ	11	Ⓐ Ⓑ Ⓒ Ⓓ
3	Ⓐ Ⓑ Ⓒ Ⓓ	6	Ⓐ Ⓑ Ⓒ Ⓓ	9	Ⓐ Ⓑ Ⓒ Ⓓ	12	Ⓐ Ⓑ Ⓒ Ⓓ

SMALL WONDERS SCORE BIG
SMALL IS TALL IN BASKETBALL

You have to be really tall, like 7' 6" Shawn Bradley or Manute Bol, to play for the National Basketball Association, right? Wrong! Little guys like 5' 3" Tyrone "Muggsy" Bogues and 5' 7" Anthony "Spud" Webb have all those big guys looking *up* to them!

Tall players have an edge when it comes to **shooting**, **blocking**, and **rebounding**. But the little guys have an edge, too! They're **quick**. They know how to pass the ball. And they can jump, too.

Take Spud Webb, for example. He can jump **nearly** four feet high. In fact, he once won the NBA Slam Dunk Contest because of his leaping ability. He also has lightning speed. In a flash, he can pass the ball to his **teammates** for an easy basket. No wonder it's so hard to **guard** Spud Webb, even if you are tall.

The NBA's "little men" are small in size but tall on the **court**. And they have their coaches, teammates, **opponents**, and fans believing that **basketball** is *not* just for the tall!

Spud Webb has proven he can play "tall."

MAIN IDEA SLAMS THE POINT HOME

What is this article mainly about?

Check the best answer.

- ❏ tall basketball players
- ❏ short basketball players
- ❏ Muggsy Bogues
- ❏ Spud Webb

48 Entertainment

ALPHABET BRINGS ORDER TO WORDS

Add the New Words to the alphabetical list.

New Words

banner

_____

_____

box

_____

_____

hammer

_____

need

_____

_____

quit

_____

_____

shop

_____

basketball
shooting
blocking
rebounding
quick
nearly
teammates
guard
court
opponents

WORDS AND MEANINGS MATCH UP

Match each New Word with its meaning. Write the letter of the meaning on the line next to the word.

_____ 1. basketball   a. fellow members of a team

_____ 2. shooting   b. almost; not quite

_____ 3. blocking   c. to move so as to keep a player from scoring

_____ 4. rebounding   d. organized game of shooting a ball through a hoop

_____ 5. quick   e. the act of catching a basketball as it bounces off the backboard or rim

_____ 6. nearly   f. the area on which a basketball game is played

_____ 7. teammates   g. the act of trying to make a basket in the game of basketball

_____ 8. guard   h. swift and speedy

_____ 9. court   i. the players on the other team

_____ 10. opponents   j. the act of trying to stop an opponent from scoring

SHORT AND TALL SENTENCES COMPLETED

Write the New Word that best completes each sentence.

1. Let's play a game of _____ after school.
2. My _____ shared the trophy with me.
3. The principal allows us to use the basketball _____ after school.
4. Our _____ find us difficult to keep up with.
5. The tall players are good at _____ because they stay beneath the basket and wait for the missed shots.
6. My _____ has been off lately, so I have not scored many points.
7. We _____ lost the game because of my playing.
8. My skills are better used when I _____ the other players.
9. Have you noticed how _____ our team is?
10. It is illegal to hit opponents when _____ their shots.

NEW WORDS

basketball   nearly
shooting   teammates
blocking   guard
rebounding   court
quick   opponents

LITTLE PREFIX MAKES BIG DIFFERENCE

A **prefix** is a word part that is added to the beginning of a root word to change its meaning. The prefix **re** means <u>again</u>.

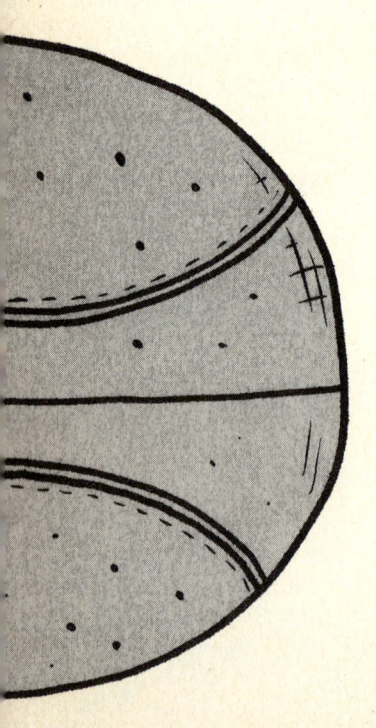

Prefix	+	Root Word	=	New Word
re	+	**build**	=	**rebuild**

Complete each sentence by adding the prefix <u>re</u> to the word below the line.

1. You will need to _____ this dress.
   order
2. Please help me _____ the stacks of papers.
   organize
3. Do you think I need to _____ the meal?
   heat
4. Jane will _____ the math problem she missed.
   figure
5. Remember to _____ the door when you leave.
   lock
6. Ben will _____ the money so there will be no mistake.
   count

AND THE CATEGORY IS . . . .

☞ Words can be grouped in **categories** to show how they go together.

Tables, **chairs**, and **beds** go together in the category <u>furniture</u>.

Circle the three words or groups of words that belong in the given category.

1. things that you would find on a <u>court</u>

   ball   end zone   players   backboard

2. places with <u>elevators</u>

   stores   planes   banks   offices

3. things you <u>plan</u>

   vacations   buildings   meetings   sleeping

4. things you do in <u>basketball</u>

   dribbling   rebounding   tackling   shooting

5. types of <u>passages</u>

   roads   halls   openings   walls

THE SHORT AND THE TALL OF IT

📝 In a group, write a report in which you compare the advantages of a short basketball team over a tall one or a tall team over a short one.

Use these questions to get your ideas rolling:

- What advantages do short players have? tall players?
- Would you rather be playing with a short team or a tall team? Why?
- What could your team do better than the other kind of team?

Use at least three of the New Words in your report.

Slam dunk the test!

TIPS FOR ALL

In dribbling, whether you're tall or small, never look at the ball!

SMALL FACTS

5' 9" Calvin Murphy once set an NBA record of 78 consecutive free throws.

KNOW THE SCORE!

READ:

- "Tall Ain't All." (*Sports Illustrated*, April 12, 1993)
- *The Story of Basketball* by Dave Anderson. (William Morrow, 1988)
- *Careers in Pro Sports* by Cordner Nelson. (Rosen Publishing Group, 1990)

IMPROVE YOUR SCORE

When more than one word could replace a blank in a sentence, be sure to choose the one that is asked for in the second sentence.

Read each set of sentences. Select the word that completes the first sentence according to the stated meaning. Fill in the circle for the answer at the bottom of the page.

1. I had to ____ the tallest player on the team.
   Which word indicates the speaker was trying to keep the opponent from shooting?
   - A gourd
   - B guess
   - C guard
   - D guide

2. He was so ____ I could not keep up with him.
   Which word indicates the opponent was fast?
   - A quick
   - B nearly
   - C almost
   - D slow

3. We play ____ once a week.
   Which word indicates a sport using a ball and hoops?
   - A football
   - B baseball
   - C basketball
   - D soccer

4. I practiced ____ for a half hour.
   Which word indicates that what was practiced was stopping an opponent's play or moving?
   - A shooting
   - B blocking
   - C rebounding
   - D basketball

5. Dad ____ missed the bus this morning.
   Which word indicates that Dad almost did not get on the bus on time?
   - A never
   - B always
   - C seldom
   - D nearly

6. The team won the game because of its ____.
   Which word indicates the game was won by the skill of seizing the basketball after it bounces off the backboard or rim of the hoop?
   - A rebounding
   - B shooting
   - C blocking
   - D basketball

Read the paragraph. Select the words that best fit in the blanks. Fill in the circles for the answers at the bottom of the page.

Our basketball team played at another school yesterday and __7__ lost the game. Our __8__ were a __9__ team, but my __10__ and I were better at __11__. We were glad for a win on their __12__.

7.
   - A now
   - B nearly
   - C newly
   - D nearby

8.
   - A opponents
   - B basketball
   - C court
   - D shooting

9.
   - A court
   - B guard
   - C quiet
   - D quick

10.
   - A basketball
   - B court
   - C opponents
   - D teammates

11.
   - A teammates
   - B shooting
   - C court
   - D opponents

12.
   - A basketball
   - B teammates
   - C court
   - D guard

ANSWERS

1 Ⓐ Ⓑ Ⓒ Ⓓ	4 Ⓐ Ⓑ Ⓒ Ⓓ	7 Ⓐ Ⓑ Ⓒ Ⓓ	10 Ⓐ Ⓑ Ⓒ Ⓓ
2 Ⓐ Ⓑ Ⓒ Ⓓ	5 Ⓐ Ⓑ Ⓒ Ⓓ	8 Ⓐ Ⓑ Ⓒ Ⓓ	11 Ⓐ Ⓑ Ⓒ Ⓓ
3 Ⓐ Ⓑ Ⓒ Ⓓ	6 Ⓐ Ⓑ Ⓒ Ⓓ	9 Ⓐ Ⓑ Ⓒ Ⓓ	12 Ⓐ Ⓑ Ⓒ Ⓓ

MYSTERIOUS GOOSE BUMPS APPEAR
PEOPLE SHIVER BUT DON'T KNOW WHY

Goose bumps or goose pimples? They're really the same thing. We get these little bumps on our skin when we're cold and **shivering**, or sometimes when we're afraid. But where did the name come from? Do geese get goose bumps? They sure do!

Geese have a network of muscles running under their **skin**. When a goose breathes in cold air, the muscles **contract**, or **tighten**. As the muscles contract, the feathers stand on end to form a warm coat. This **insulation** helps to keep in the goose's body heat.

Just below the **surface** of your skin, each hair root is encircled by a **follicle**, or a small group of **cells**. A special muscle is attached to most hair follicles. When you get cold, nerves in your skin **communicate** a message to your brain. Your brain sends a message to the muscles around your hair follicles telling them to tighten just as a goose's muscles do. The **involuntary**, or automatic, tightening pulls on each tiny hair. This creates the bumpy appearance of the skin.

So next time you get goose bumps, you might just want to remember this hair-raising tale.

SHIVERING SEQUENCE
What's the sequence?
Number the events in order.

____ a muscle contracts

____ your brain tells your muscles to tighten

____ you feel cold

____ nerves communicate a message to your brain

ALPHABET PUTS WORDS IN ORDER

Add the New Words to the alphabetical list.

NEW WORDS		
shivering	bluebird	interior
skin	_____	_____
contract	_____	_____
tighten	complain	shock
insulation	_____	_____
surface	_____	_____
follicle	_____	_____
cells	football	sweeten
communicate		
involuntary	_____	_____

WORDS MATCH WITH MEANINGS

Match each New Word with its meaning. Write the letter of the meaning on the line next to the word.

___ 1. shivering   a. very tiny units of living matter

___ 2. skin   b. to pass on information

___ 3. contract   c. automatic and uncontrolled

___ 4. tighten   d. outer covering of an animal's or a person's body

___ 5. insulation   e. a layer of material that protects

___ 6. surface   f. the top part of anything

___ 7. follicle   g. to strain; become taut

___ 8. cells   h. the sac in which a hair root sits

___ 9. communicate   i. shaking from cold or fear

___ 10. involuntary   j. to tighten or become smaller

NEW WORDS

shivering
skin
contract
tighten
insulation
surface
follicle
cells
communicate
involuntary

WORDS WARM UP SENTENCES

Write the New Word that best completes each sentence.

1. The _____ in your body are so small that you cannot see them.
2. A sneeze is an _____ action.
3. I was _____ because of the cold.
4. Do not let dirt get into a hair _____ .
5. Your _____ will be healthy if you keep it clean.
6. I want to _____ with your parents about your improvement.
7. My jacket acts as _____ against the cold winds.
8. You will be warmer if you _____ your scarf around your neck.
9. The _____ of the lake was frozen solid.
10. You may feel pain when your muscles _____ .

HOMONYMS SURE SOUND ALIKE

☛ **Homonyms** are words that sound alike but have different spellings and meanings.

there and **their**

feet and **feat**

Draw lines to match the homonyms.

1. herd   a. sale
2. plain   b. sells
3. sail   c. plane
4. cells   d. heard

Use these homonyms to complete the sentences.

5. Mary _____ the news on the radio.
6. Dad learned to _____ on Crystal Lake.
7. We looked at the _____ under the microscope.
8. The store will have a _____ on clothes this week.

YOU GET THE PICTURE!

Write the New Word that is suggested by each picture.

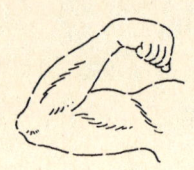

NEW WORDS

shivering	surface
skin	follicle
contract	communicate
insulation	involuntary

1. _____

2. _____

3. _____

4. _____

5. _____

6. _____

7. _____

8. _____

HAIR-RAISING FACTS

✲ When an animal is scared, it gets goose bumps. Why? Goose bumps cause its hair to stand on end and puff out. This makes the scared animal look larger and more dangerous.

✲ Naked geese were a common sight years ago. The geese were plucked four or five times a year for their soft, downy feathers. Goose down is still used today in pillows, quilts, and warm jackets.

FOR MORE GOOSE BUMPS READ:

- *Animal Amazing* by Judith Herbst. (Atheneum, 1991)
- *I've Got Goose Pimples: Our Great Expressions and How They Came to Be* by Marvin Vanoni. (Morrow, 1989)

☆ BUMPS IN THE NIGHT ☆

Sometimes we get goose bumps when we are scared. Write a story about a time when you were really afraid.

Use these questions to help jog your memory:
- What caused you to be afraid?
- How did you handle this situation?
- What did you learn from this experience?

Use at least three of the New Words in your story.

Don't be scared to take the test!

SECRETS TO SUCCESS ON TESTS

Be sure to erase any pencil marks that you made outside the answer circle.

Read each group of words. Select the word or words that mean the same as the underlined word. Fill in the circle for the answer at the bottom of the page.

1 cold and <u>shivering</u>
- A shaking
- B talking
- C sweating
- D thinking

2 <u>contract</u> the muscle
- A expand
- B draw together
- C pull apart
- D relax

3 <u>involuntary</u> movement
- A free
- B not done on purpose
- C fast
- D not done well

4 <u>tighten</u> the grip
- A turn
- B loosen
- C hold firmly
- D make bigger

5 hair <u>follicle</u>
- A tiny sac in skin
- B small muscle
- C style
- D cut

6 living <u>cells</u>
- A windows
- B rooms
- C units of living matter
- D units of length

7 below the <u>surface</u>
- A underneath
- B underside
- C outside
- D inside

8 thick <u>skin</u>
- A muscle
- B covering
- C feathers
- D fur

Read each sentence. Select the answer that best completes each one. Fill in the circle for the answer at the bottom of the page.

9 Muscles lie just below the ____ .
- A follicle
- B skin
- C cells
- D voluntary

10 There is rock just below the ____ of the Earth.
- A sand
- B skin
- C gravel
- D surface

11 Speaking clearly helps you ____ with your audience.
- A insulate
- B message
- C communicate
- D compromise

12 Feathers act as ____ for the bird.
- A surface
- B communication
- C contract
- D insulation

ANSWERS

1 Ⓐ Ⓑ Ⓒ Ⓓ	4 Ⓐ Ⓑ Ⓒ Ⓓ	7 Ⓐ Ⓑ Ⓒ Ⓓ	10 Ⓐ Ⓑ Ⓒ Ⓓ
2 Ⓐ Ⓑ Ⓒ Ⓓ	5 Ⓐ Ⓑ Ⓒ Ⓓ	8 Ⓐ Ⓑ Ⓒ Ⓓ	11 Ⓐ Ⓑ Ⓒ Ⓓ
3 Ⓐ Ⓑ Ⓒ Ⓓ	6 Ⓐ Ⓑ Ⓒ Ⓓ	9 Ⓐ Ⓑ Ⓒ Ⓓ	12 Ⓐ Ⓑ Ⓒ Ⓓ

WIDOW GOES ON BLIND DATE
MATE NEVER SEEN AGAIN

The black widow spider is black, and she is a **widow**. Her **mate** dies soon after they meet. Sometimes she **dines** on him. She is a **wicked** widow. The black widow is one of the few **common** spiders that can hurt people. Her bite can even **cause** people to die.

Where do black widows live? They make webs in dark, dry places. Watch out for them when you go into an **attic** or other dark, dry place.

Here is how to tell if a spider is a black widow. A black widow could fit on a penny. Her back part is bigger than the rest of the body. It is round and **shiny**. Some black widows have brightly colored marks on top. Others are almost all black.

There is one sure sign of a black widow. She has a red mark under her body. The mark is in the **shape** of an **hourglass**. Do not pick up a black, shiny spider to look for this mark. This lady can be a killer.

"One look at her and I knew my time was up!"
says unsuspecting date.

STORY SPINS SEQUENCE WEB

Which happens first in the story?

Check the best answer.
❑ The black widow dies.
❑ The black widow's mate dies.
❑ A black widow could stand on a penny.
❑ The black widow can live in an attic.

ALPHABETICALLY SPEAKING

New Words

common, mate, wicked, hourglass, dines, shape, widow, attic, shiny, cause

Add the following New Words to the alphabetical list below.

attest _____

cattle _____

complain _____

house _____

shame _____

ship _____

MEANINGS DISCOVERED

Match each New Word below with its meaning. Write the letter on the line next to the word.

____ 1. widow

____ 2. mate

____ 3. dines

____ 4. common

____ 5. cause

____ 6. attic

____ 7. shiny

____ 8. shape

____ 9. hourglass

____ 10. wicked

a. room or space just below the roof of a house

b. giving off light or reflecting light; bright

c. to make happen; bring about

d. bad or harmful on purpose; evil

e. of the usual kind; ordinary

f. a device for measuring time by the trickling of sand from one glass bulb through a small opening to another bulb below it

g. the way something looks because of its outline; outer form; figure

h. eats a meal

i. one part of a pair

j. a woman whose husband has died and who has not married again

SENTENCE HOLES FILLED AT LAST

New Words

attic, widow, cause, wicked, mate, shape, shiny, hourglass, common, dines

Write the New Words that best complete the sentences.

1. The _____ has lived by herself since her _____ died ten years ago.

2. Mary found an old _____ in the _____ of her grandmother's house.

3. Did the _____ witch _____ the princess to sleep for fifty years?

4. Mrs. Wong _____ at that restaurant. It is quite _____ to see her there.

5. Luis found a bright, _____ piece of metal that has a _____ like a heart.

LESS MEANS MORE WITH SUFFIXES

A **suffix** is a word part that can be added to the end of a root word. Adding a suffix changes the meaning of the root word. For example, the suffix **less** means <u>without</u>.

Root Word	Suffix	New Word
hair	+ less =	hairless

Complete the sentences by adding the suffix less to the root word that is underlined.

1. If air is without <u>shape</u>, air is _____ .
2. If a liquid is without <u>color</u>, it is a _____ liquid.
3. If an idea is without <u>sense</u>, the idea is _____ .
4. If your brother is without <u>fear</u>, you have a _____ brother.
5. If a bus is without <u>power</u>, the bus is _____ .
6. If a bug is without <u>harm</u>, it is a _____ bug.
7. If your dinner is without <u>flavor</u>, the dinner is _____ .
8. If you cross the street without <u>care</u>, you are _____ .
9. If a tool is without <u>use</u>, it is _____ .
10. If a stamp is without <u>worth</u>, it is a _____ stamp.

NO MORE CROSS WORDS!

Use the New Words to complete the crossword puzzle.

Across

1. outer form
3. woman whose husband has died
5. bring about; make happen
6. space below the roof of a house
7. male or female of a pair
8. eats dinner
9. giving off light; bright

Down

2. device for measuring time
4. bad on purpose
5. of the usual kind

Spider Proves Dangerous — That's a Fact

Look up *tarantula* in the encyclopedia or in another book to find information about this large, hairy spider. Write a short report about what you discover.

Think about these questions to help you get started.

- What does the tarantula look like?
- Where do tarantulas live?
- What do they eat?

Use at least three New Words in your report.

SPIN A WEB OF YOUR OWN!

Read:

- *Amazing Spiders* by Alexandra Parsons. (Knopf, 1990)

- *Extremely Weird Spiders* by Sarah Lovett. (J. Muir, 1991)

ITSY BITSY SPIDER FACTS

In any field on any nice day, there could be two million spiders!

Spin on over to the test.

SECRETS TO SUCCESS ON TESTS

When looking for a word that means the same as another, don't be fooled by a choice that means the opposite.

Read each group of words. Select the answer that means the same as the underlined word. Fill in the circle for the answer at the bottom of the page.

1. a <u>common</u> mistake
   - A terrible
   - B careless
   - C everyday
   - D rare

2. <u>cause</u> the accident
   - A see
   - B hear
   - C bring about
   - D run from

3. <u>shape</u> of the ball
   - A color
   - B form
   - C thrown
   - D circle

4. a <u>shiny</u> penny
   - A bright
   - B new
   - C good
   - D dull

5. the <u>wicked</u> witch
   - A old
   - B friendly
   - C stooped
   - D evil

6. a broken <u>hourglass</u>
   - A window
   - B mug
   - C timer
   - D watch

Read each sentence. Select the word that best completes the sentence. Fill in the circle for the answer at the bottom of the page

7. Our family _____ at six o'clock every evening.
   - A writes
   - B talks
   - C travels
   - D dines

8. The family pictures were in a trunk in the _____.
   - A hourglass
   - B attic
   - C kitchen
   - D hole

9. The elderly man depends upon his _____ for care.
   - A history
   - B automobile
   - C widow
   - D mate

10. The _____ lived alone after her husband died.
    - A wiggle
    - B window
    - C widow
    - D wonder

11. You have made a _____ error in your test.
    - A shiny
    - B common
    - C wicked
    - D mate

12. A square is a _____ with four sides that are the same length.
    - A shape
    - B mate
    - C common
    - D cause

THIS GORILLA CAN TALK TO YOU

Koko is a very smart **gorilla**. When she was young, her keepers wanted to see if she could learn to talk. But, gorillas cannot make all the sounds that are needed for **normal speech**. **Therefore**, her keepers taught her to use sign language.

After some years, Koko learned six hundred words. Koko gets **messages** across in the same way as those who are **deaf** or those who are not able to talk. She even made up her own ways to say things. She once called a **pill** a candy bean.

One day she told the keepers she wanted a kitten for her birthday. The keepers got her one. She named the kitten "All Ball" because it had no tail. She **combed**, kissed, **tickled,** and talked to the kitten. When All Ball died, Koko seemed sad for two months. Then, Koko got another kitten and was happy again.

Koko also liked to play with a doll. It looked like a baby gorilla. She would **form** its hands to make sign language. If Koko had a real baby gorilla, do you think she would teach it how to talk?

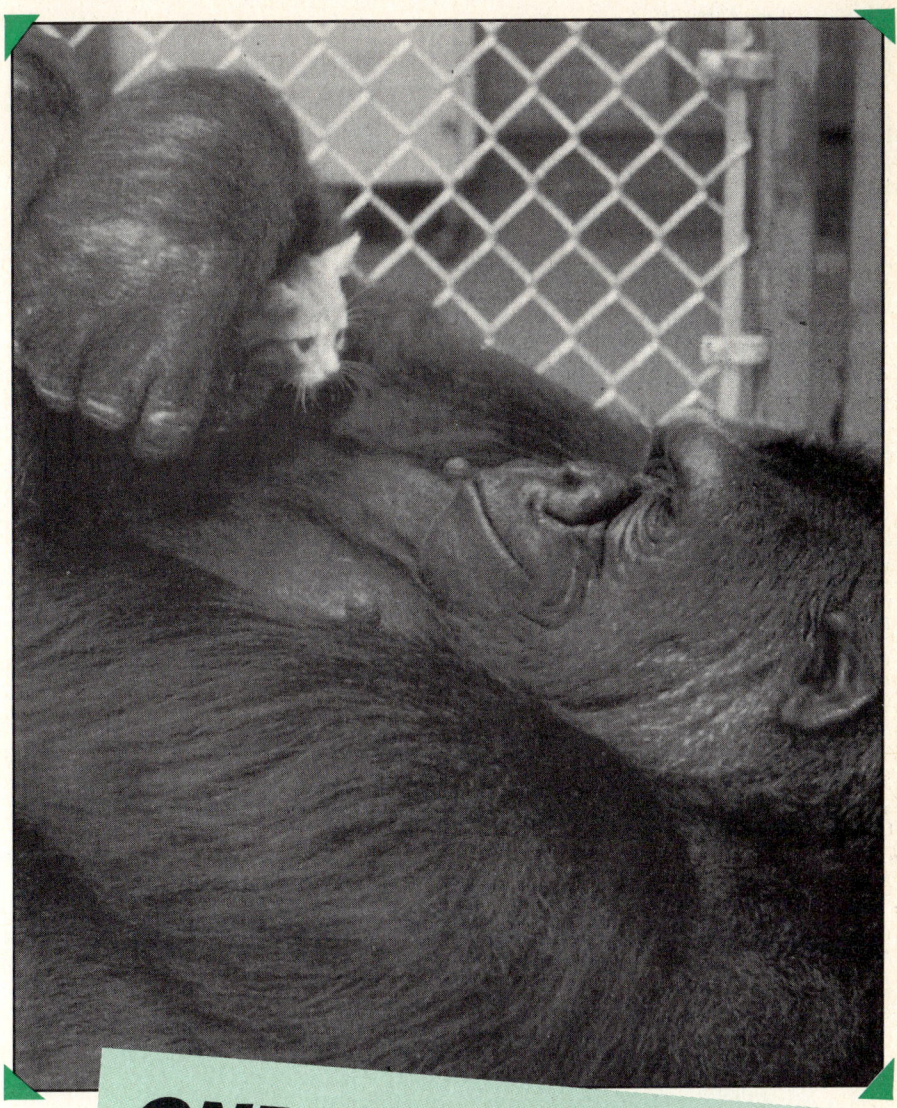

ONE THING LEADS TO ANOTHER

What happened first in the story? Check the best answer.

○ Koko asked for a present.
○ Koko got another kitten.
○ Koko was sad for a long time.
○ Koko learned to use sign language.

GOING APE FOR THE ALPHABET

Add the New Words to the alphabetical list below.

NEW WORDS

gorilla
speech
messages
pill
tickled
normal
therefore
deaf
combed
form

color

_____

_____

dear

_____

fort

_____

_____

metal

_____

nose

_____

_____

spell

_____

_____

WORDS SEEK MEANINGS

Match each New Word with its meaning. Write the letter of the meaning next to the word.

____ 1. gorilla

____ 2. normal

____ 3. speech

____ 4. deaf

____ 5. pill

____ 6. combed

____ 7. tickled

____ 8. form

____ 9. therefore

____ 10. messages

a. smoothed, arranged, or cleaned with a comb

b. the act or way of speaking

c. not able to hear or hardly able to hear

d. to give a certain shape to

e. touched or stroked lightly, as with a finger or feather, so as to cause twitching or laughing

f. a little ball or capsule of medicine to be swallowed whole

g. the largest and the strongest of the apes, found in Africa

h. pieces of news, requests, facts, sent from one person to another

i. agreeing with a standard or norm; natural; usual

j. for this or that reason; as a result

INCOMPLETE SENTENCES JUST DON'T ADD UP

Write the New Words that best complete the sentences.

1. My sister is _____ in both ears.

2. _____ , our family has learned sign language.

3. My temperature was higher than _____ when I had the flu.

4. I had to take a _____ four times a day.

5. Danny's _____ is hard to understand.

6. A special teacher will help him learn how to _____ his words.

7. Mother _____ my hair before I had my picture taken.

8. It _____ my neck and made me laugh.

9. There were several important _____ on the police radio.

10. A _____ from the zoo was on the loose.

MULTIPLE MEANINGS COULD SPELL TROUBLE

Many words have more than one meaning. **Context clues** in sentences can help you determine the meanings of these words.

top can mean a toy
top can mean above

The words speech and row each have more than one meaning. Write the letter of the best meaning on the line next to each sentence.

speech
a. the act of speaking
b. a talk given in public

row
a. a number of things in a line
b. to move a boat with oars

____ 1. Many Americans listened to the President's speech on the radio.

____ 2. A person who lisps may not have clear speech.

____ 3. Ben sits in the second row from the back.

____ 4. Sarah will row the boat for a while.

65

IF YOU COULD TALK TO THE ANIMALS

Have you ever talked to a gorilla at the zoo? What did you say? Write a short paragraph telling what you and a gorilla might say to each other.

The following questions will give you some ideas.
- Does the gorilla like living in his cage?
- What are his or her favorite foods?
- What might a gorilla ask you?

Use at least three New Words in your paragraph.

WORD SEARCH IS MONKEY BUSINESS

Find the hidden New Words and circle them.

```
M E S S E E C T M H S
N C O M B E D I E O R
A L D E N A F C S G O
R I L F O P L K S A T
H E G O R I L L A R E
F O E R M L S E G C S
O M B M A L A D E G P
S A R T L T D O S R E
M F T H E R E F O R E
T H E R E F A R M A C
L N O R L E F D L L H
```

LEARN MORE ABOUT GORILLAS IN YOUR SPARE TIME

READ:

- *With Love From Koko* by Faith McNulty. (Scholastic, 1990)

- *Koko's Kitten* by Francine Patterson. (Scholastic, 1985)

- *Gorillas* by Althea Braithwaite. (Longman Group USA, 1988)

GREAT GORILLA Facts

The male leader of a gorilla family group is called a silverback. He can have the strength of four to eight strong men!

New Words

combed	tickled
therefore	form
normal	messages
gorilla	speech
deaf	pill

Swing on to the test!

TEST-TAKING SECRETS REVEALED

Go back to the story to see how the key word is used there. This will help you to see its meaning.

Complete each definition with the best word or group of words. Fill in the circle for the answer at the bottom of the page.

1 A <u>normal</u> day is one that is—
   - A regular
   - B angry
   - C long
   - D unusual

2 <u>Combed</u> means—
   - A braided
   - B smoothed
   - C curled
   - D washed

3 To be <u>deaf</u> means to be unable to—
   - A walk
   - B call
   - C hear
   - D speak

4 To <u>form</u> means to—
   - A shape
   - B throw
   - C catch
   - D toss

5 <u>Speech</u> is the act of—
   - A hearing
   - B walking
   - C speaking
   - D seeing

6 To be <u>tickled</u> is to be—
   - A shoved aside
   - B touched playfully
   - C hugged
   - D spanked

Read each set of sentences. Select the answer that best completes the second sentence in the set. Fill in the circle for the answer at the bottom of the page.

7 I, <u>therefore</u>, will not go. <u>Therefore</u> means—
   - A at this time
   - B at that place
   - C as a result
   - D for some time

8 My favorite animal at the zoo is the <u>gorilla</u>. A <u>gorilla</u> is a kind of—
   - A lion
   - B bird
   - C elephant
   - D ape

9 I sent <u>messages</u> to him while he was away. <u>Messages</u> means—
   - A clothes
   - B information
   - C packages
   - D food

10 He swallowed the <u>pill</u> with a little water. <u>Pill</u> means—
   - A food
   - B medicine
   - C fruit
   - D candy

11 That was a <u>normal</u> reaction to the event. <u>Normal</u> means—
   - A happy
   - B silent
   - C noisy
   - D natural

12 She watched the artist <u>form</u> a statue from the ice. <u>Form</u> means—
   - A draw
   - B paint
   - C make
   - D melt

ANSWERS

1 Ⓐ Ⓑ Ⓒ Ⓓ	4 Ⓐ Ⓑ Ⓒ Ⓓ	7 Ⓐ Ⓑ Ⓒ Ⓓ	10 Ⓐ Ⓑ Ⓒ Ⓓ
2 Ⓐ Ⓑ Ⓒ Ⓓ	5 Ⓐ Ⓑ Ⓒ Ⓓ	8 Ⓐ Ⓑ Ⓒ Ⓓ	11 Ⓐ Ⓑ Ⓒ Ⓓ
3 Ⓐ Ⓑ Ⓒ Ⓓ	6 Ⓐ Ⓑ Ⓒ Ⓓ	9 Ⓐ Ⓑ Ⓒ Ⓓ	12 Ⓐ Ⓑ Ⓒ Ⓓ

ICEBERGS LURK IN OCEAN

Icebergs are very large pieces of ice that float in the ocean. The ice is so heavy that most of it is under the water. Only a small piece of an iceberg shows above the water. The part above the water may not seem very tiny, though. It may stick out of the water as tall as a fifteen-story building! Some icebergs have been fifty miles long.

Although it may sound strange, icebergs are formed in the warmest times of the year. In very cold areas, **thick** ice is **frozen** on land in winter. In warmer weather, the ice begins to **melt** and slide toward the sea. When the ice breaks apart and crashes into the sea, an iceberg is formed.

In bad **weather**, icebergs can be dangerous. Ships are sometimes **damaged** when they ram into an iceberg. A famous **wreck** happened in 1912. The sailors on a great new ship, the *Titanic*, **received** some **warnings** about icebergs. But they did nothing. The *Titanic* sank when it hit an iceberg. Over one thousand five hundred people lost their lives.

SEQUENCE FROZEN IN STORY

Which of these happens first? *Check the best answer.*

❏ The ice slides toward the sea.

❏ The ice starts to melt.

❏ The ice falls into the sea.

❏ Thick ice forms on land.

68 Nature

ALPHABET PUTS WORDS ON ICE

Add the New Words to the alphabetical list below.

New Words
iceberg
thick
melt
wreck
damaged
although
frozen
weather
warnings
received

aloud
_____
_____
dance
_____
_____
icicle
_____

member
_____
recipe
_____
thin
_____
_____
_____

WORDS ADRIFT WITHOUT MEANING

Match each New Word below with its meaning. Write the letter on the line next to the word.

___ 1. icebergs
___ 2. although
___ 3. thick
___ 4. frozen
___ 5. melt
___ 6. weather
___ 7. wreck
___ 8. warnings
___ 9. damaged
___ 10. received

a. to have taken or got what was given or sent
b. in spite of the fact; even; though
c. the remains of something that has been destroyed or badly damaged
d. injured or harmed in a way that results in a loss of health or value
e. great in width or depth from side to side; not thin
f. things that tell of danger; advice to be careful
g. masses of ice broken off from a glacier and floating in the sea
h. to change from a solid to a liquid by heat
i. the conditions outside at any time and place with regard to such things as temperature, sunshine, and rainfall
j. turned into or covered with ice

69

WORDS FINISH SENTENCES

Write the New Words that best complete the sentences.

1. We called 911 after we saw the car _____ .
2. The ice cubes were not completely _____ .
3. _____ I was tired, I raced to the finish line.
4. We hoped that the sun would _____ the snow on the sidewalk.
5. Dad thinks we will have stormy _____ tomorrow.
6. There were small _____ floating near the ship.
7. We heard winter storm _____ on TV.
8. Mom cut me a _____ slice of cake.
9. Sarah _____ many gifts for her birthday.
10. Everyone carefully inspected the _____ building after the tornado.

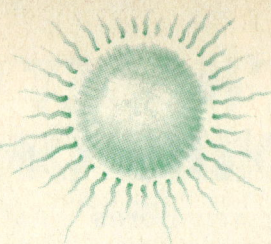

New Words
icebergs
thick
melt
wreck
damaged
although
frozen
weather
warnings
received

WORD ENDINGS ARE JUST THE TIP OF THE ICEBERG!

☞ **Endings** can be added to many words. Sometimes the spelling of a word must be changed when an ending is added.

If a word ends in a consonant and y, change the y to i before adding er or est.

funny + er = funnier

If a word with a short vowel ends in a single consonant, double the final consonant before adding er or est.

big + est = biggest

If a word ends in e, drop the e before adding er or est.

safe + est = safest

Add the endings er and est to the words listed.

Word	er	est
1. easy	_____	_____
2. flat	_____	_____
3. white	_____	_____
4. lazy	_____	_____
5. hot	_____	_____
6. nice	_____	_____

SECRET CODE
REVEALS NEW NAME FOR THE TITANIC

Break the coded message below to discover the nickname for the British ship, the *Titanic*, that sank in 1912.

Write the New Word for each meaning on the lines to discover the letter/number code.

1. even though   __ __ __ __ __ __ __ __
                 10 18 3 19 22 1 6 19

2. signs of danger   __ __ __ __ __ __ __
                    24 10 4 11 13 11 6 14

3. not thin   __ __ __ __ __
              3 19 13 2 20

4. masses of ice   __ __ __ __ __ __ __
                  13 2 15 26 15 4 6 14

DISCOVER THE SECRET NAME
Now write the coded letters below to find the answer.

__ __ __
3 19 15

__ __ __ __ __ __ __ __ __
1 11 14 13 11 20 10 26 18 15

__ __ __ __ __ __
3 13 3 10 11 13 2

READ MORE
ABOUT THIS COOL SUBJECT
- *The Titanic* by Tom Stacey. (Lucent Books, 1989)
- *Icebergs and Glaciers* by Seymour Simon. (Morrow, 1987)
- *Icebergs and Their Voyages* by Gwen M. Schultz. (Morrow, 1975)

CHECK OUT THIS VIDEO
- *Iceland River Challenge.* (National Geographic Society, 1986)

SHOULD THE TITANIC RISE AGAIN?

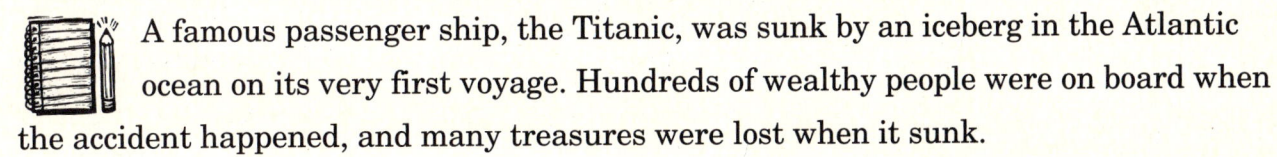

A famous passenger ship, the Titanic, was sunk by an iceberg in the Atlantic ocean on its very first voyage. Hundreds of wealthy people were on board when the accident happened, and many treasures were lost when it sunk.

In 1985, the Titanic was found deep in the Atlantic Ocean. The water is so deep where the ship was found that only robots with cameras can reach it. It would be very dangerous and expensive to try to rescue the treasures on board the ship.

Write a short paragraph telling if you think people should try bringing up the Titanic and its treasures.

The following questions will guide you in writing your paragraph.

- Would it be worth the cost to bring up the Titanic?
- What do you think would be found on the old ship?
- Why would it be dangerous to bring up the Titanic?

Use at least three New Words in your paragraph.

Be cool! Take the test!

SCORE HIGHER ON TESTS

Fill in the whole answer circle, but do not spend too much time on each one.

Read each group of words. Select the answer that means the opposite of the underlined word. Fill in the circle for the answer at the bottom of the page.

1 a frozen pond

   A icy   C deep
   B shallow   D thawed

2 the thick blanket

   A soft   C heavy
   B thin   D warm

3 received a gift

   A gave   C saw
   B wanted   D bought

4 melt the ice

   A move   C thaw
   B chop   D freeze

Read the paragraphs. Select the words that best fit in the blanks. Fill in the circles for the answers at the bottom of the page.

Every year ice breaks off from the land of Antarctica forming __5__. These __6__ slabs of ice float in the water until they __7__. __8__ they are beautiful to see, they can be dangerous to ships.

Even though we had __9__ that the __10__ was going to turn bad, we still went driving in the car. Before too long we passed a __11__ on the road. We were glad to see that the car was only slightly __12__.

5 A warnings
   B icebergs
   C weather
   D islands

6 A light
   B shiny
   C thick
   D small

7 A freeze
   B land
   C melt
   D sink

8 A However
   B Although
   C Anyway
   D Yet

9 A received
   B warnings
   C weather
   D secrets

10 A weather
   B damage
   C wreck
   D child

11 A car
   B damage
   C iceberg
   D wreck

12 A received
   B warned
   C damaged
   D melted

ANSWERS

1 Ⓐ Ⓑ Ⓒ Ⓓ	4 Ⓐ Ⓑ Ⓒ Ⓓ	7 Ⓐ Ⓑ Ⓒ Ⓓ	10 Ⓐ Ⓑ Ⓒ Ⓓ
2 Ⓐ Ⓑ Ⓒ Ⓓ	5 Ⓐ Ⓑ Ⓒ Ⓓ	8 Ⓐ Ⓑ Ⓒ Ⓓ	11 Ⓐ Ⓑ Ⓒ Ⓓ
3 Ⓐ Ⓑ Ⓒ Ⓓ	6 Ⓐ Ⓑ Ⓒ Ⓓ	9 Ⓐ Ⓑ Ⓒ Ⓓ	12 Ⓐ Ⓑ Ⓒ Ⓓ

WHO IS THIS MAN ON THE FIVE DOLLAR BILL?

Look at the face on a five dollar bill. It is the face of Abraham Lincoln. In 1861, he became the 16th **president** of the United States.

When Abraham Lincoln was young, people found that he could be **trusted**. He always told the **truth**, and he did not **steal**. Because he was **honest**, he got the nickname "Honest Abe."

Once Abe was working in a little store. He made a **mistake** when he gave a woman change. When Abe found out he was wrong, he **decided** to do the right thing. He walked three miles to give back the six cents to the woman.

Later, Abe **borrowed** money to start a store with a friend. The **business** did not do well. They could not pay back what they had borrowed. Abe worked many years to pay back the money. He really was "Honest Abe."

When you look at a one-cent **coin**, think of Abraham Lincoln. He was honest down to the penny.

Matthew Brady took this picture in 1864. It is the same photo used today on the five dollar bill.

SEQUENCE KEEPS STORY IN ORDER

What happened after Abe found out that he had made a mistake?

Check the best answer.
- ❑ Abe gave a woman six cents.
- ❑ Abe worked to pay back the money.
- ❑ Abe decided to do what was right.
- ❑ Abe made a mistake in giving change.

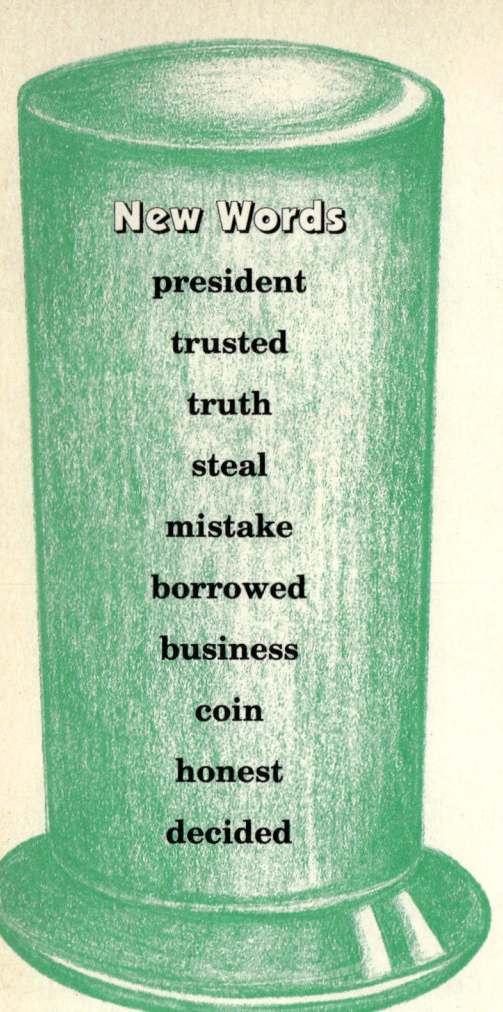

THE AMAZING ALPHABET

New Words
- president
- trusted
- truth
- steal
- mistake
- borrowed
- business
- coin
- honest
- decided

☞ In the dictionary, **guide words** at the top of the page show the first and last entries on the page. All other entries on the page are in alphabetical order between those words.

Write the New Words in alphabetical order under the correct guide words.

born/cold

_____

_____

_____

collect/honor

_____

_____

_____

hop/prevent

_____

_____

prey/try

_____

_____

_____

WORDS AND MEANINGS UNITED

Match each New Word with its meaning. Write the letter of the meaning on the line next to the word.

____ 1. mistake
____ 2. honest
____ 3. steal
____ 4. business
____ 5. borrowed
____ 6. coin
____ 7. president
____ 8. trusted
____ 9. decided
____ 10. truth

a. the head of the United States government; the highest officer of a company, club, college, and so on
b. believed in or depended upon as a result of being honest or fair
c. a piece of metal money having a certain value
d. truthful; capable of being trusted
e. to take away secretly and without permission
f. chose after some thought; made up one's mind
g. an idea, answer, or act that is wrong; error or blunder
h. used for awhile with the understanding one would return it later
i. a commercial establishment such as a store; one's work or occupation
j. what is true, honest, sincere, accurate

MYSTERY SOLVED! MISSING WORDS FOUND

Write the New Words that best complete the sentences.

1. Beth's dad wanted to start his own _____ .

2. He _____ to open a shoe store.

3. Willy _____ a quarter from his sister.

4. He put the _____ in the candy machine.

5. Kim was elected class _____ .

6. She was admired because she always told the _____ .

7. Never _____ things from other people.

8. If you take things that are not yours, you will not be _____ .

9. Cheryl told Mrs. James that she had made a _____ in grading her paper.

10. Mrs. James was proud of Cheryl for being so _____ .

THE TRUTH ABOUT PREFIXES

A **prefix** is a word part that can be added to the beginning of a root word. Adding a prefix changes the meaning of the root word. For example, the prefix **dis** means <u>not</u>.

Prefix	Root Word	New Word
dis +	**belief** =	**disbelief**

Add the prefix <u>dis</u> to each underlined word. Write the word on the line.

MEANING   NEW WORD

1. to not <u>trust</u>   _____

2. to not <u>like</u>   _____

3. to not <u>obey</u>   _____

4. to not <u>continue</u>   _____

Now choose the best words to complete the sentences below.

5. People who _____ the law will be punished. (distrust, disobey)

6. If you tell lies, people will _____ you. (disobey, distrust)

7. I'm upset because my favorite TV show was _____ . (discontinued, disagreed)

8. My dad _____ mowing the grass every week. (dislikes, disconnects)

WORD MIX-UP
STRAIGHTENED OUT

Unscramble the New Words and write them on the lines.

New Words
- trusted
- decided
- honest
- coin
- president
- steal
- mistake
- borrowed
- business
- truth

1. deprintse _____
2. hurtt _____
3. doorrewb _____
4. sthone _____
5. kitsame _____
6. sunibess _____
7. struted _____
8. least _____
9. oinc _____
10. cdddeie _____

READ MORE ABOUT THIS HONEST MAN

- *A Picture Book of Abraham Lincoln* by David Adler. (Holiday House, 1989)
- *Lincoln: A Photo Biography* by Russell Freedman. (Clarion Books, 1987)
- *Just a few Words, Mr. Lincoln: The Story of the Gettysburg Address* by Jean Fritz. (Grossett and Dunlap, 1993)

BAA - BAA

Lincoln's youngest son, Tad, had a goat that slept on his bed in the White House.

THE MAN WHO COULDN'T LIE
ANOTHER HONEST PRESIDENT

Look at the picture to the right. The picture illustrates George Washington cutting down a cherry tree. It is a legend that people liked to tell when describing how honest George Washington was. Ask your teacher or librarian to tell you the story, or read about the legend of George Washington and the cherry tree. Then write a short paragraph retelling the story.

The following questions will help you get started.
- How old was George when he cut down the tree?
- What did he use to cut down the cherry tree?
- What did he say when he was asked who cut down the tree?

Use at least three New Words in your paragraph.

76

Honestly, you can take the test!

TEST-DAY TIPS TOLD

Be careful of answers that look or sound alike. Say the words to yourself.

Read each sentence. Select the word that best completes the sentence. Fill in the circle for the answer at the bottom of the page.

1. The class _____ gave a talk about helping with the project.
   - A pride
   - B president
   - C press
   - D position

2. Because she is honest, you can always depend on Katy to tell the _____.
   - A message
   - B story
   - C information
   - D truth

3. Once I _____ to go, I had to hurry to get ready.
   - A trusted
   - B decided
   - C borrowed
   - D dressed

4. A new _____ is starting up in that office building.
   - A mistake
   - B president
   - C coin
   - D business

5. The robber tried to _____ the money.
   - A steel
   - B steal
   - C stray
   - D store

6. I tried to erase the _____ on my test paper.
   - A mistake
   - B coin
   - C business
   - D truth

Read each set of sentences. Select the word that completes the first sentence according to the stated meaning. Fill in the circle for the answer at the bottom of the page.

7. Your parents _____ you to do the right thing. Which word indicates that your parents believed in you?
   - A trusted
   - B truth
   - C honest
   - D decided

8. The dime is our country's smallest _____. Which word indicates a flat piece of metal money?
   - A dollar
   - B bill
   - C token
   - D coin

9. I had _____ his lawn mower to cut the grass. Which word indicates that the mower was loaned to the speaker?
   - A decided
   - B borrowed
   - C trusted
   - D shared

10. _____ answers will take care of the problems. Which word indicates that the answers should be the truth.
    - A Sharp
    - B Trusted
    - C Honest
    - D Quick

11. Michael was named _____ of his company. Which word indicates that Michael became the leader of his company?
    - A business
    - B president
    - C truth
    - D honest

12. When you have _____ what you want, let me know. Which word indicates that you have to make up your mind?
    - A trusted
    - B borrowed
    - C decided
    - D taken

ROADRUNNER
ALWAYS ON THE MOVE

A roadrunner is a strange bird. It lives in the hot, dry parts of North America. This large, **speckled** bird looks like a **skinny** chicken with a long thin bill and a **narrow** tail.

The roadrunner hardly ever flies, but it runs fast with the help of its wings. It pulls out its wings and takes long steps as it **glides** along **swiftly**. The roadrunner can outrun most people. It can get away from almost anything that chases it. It can dart this way and that. To change **directions** quickly, it just flips out one wing. It sails across deep **ditches** and glides off **cliffs** to get away.

The bird's strange appetite makes it helpful to people. It might have spiders or grasshoppers for breakfast. It **gulps** down a **lizard** or a mouse for lunch. It may eat a snake for a filling supper. If you ever ride through roadrunner country, look for this strange but useful bird.

CAREFUL READING HELPS DETERMINE CAUSE

Why do people think of the roadrunner as a useful bird? *Check the best answer.*

○ It makes a good pet.
○ It eats things people do not like.
○ It can dart this way and that.
○ It can run faster than they can.

78 Nature

RACE THROUGH THE DICTIONARY WITH GUIDE WORDS

👉 In the dictionary, **guide words** at the top of the page show the first and last entries on the page. All other entries on the page are in alphabetical order between those words.

Write the New Words in alphabetical order under the correct guide words.

click/dive

_____

_____

_____

gun/nasty

_____

_____

divide/gum

_____

_____

_____

nation/swim

_____

_____

_____

NEW WORDS

speckled
skinny
narrow
cliffs
swiftly
ditches
glides
gulps
lizard
directions

PERFECT MATCH FOUND BETWEEN WORDS AND MEANINGS

Match each New Word below with its meaning. Write the letter of the meaning on the line next to the word.

____ 1. gulps

____ 2. lizard

____ 3. skinny

____ 4. speckled

____ 5. directions

____ 6. cliffs

____ 7. swiftly

____ 8. ditches

____ 9. narrow

____ 10. glides

a. in a fast manner; quickly

b. moves along in a smooth and easy way, as in skating

c. a reptile with a long, slender body and tail, scaly skin, and four legs

d. very lean or thin

e. long, narrow openings dug in the earth; trenches

f. having small marks or spots

g. high, steep faces of rock that go down sharply with little or no slope

h. small in width; less wide than usual

i. the points toward which things face, or the lines along which things move or lie

j. swallows in a hurried or greedy way

79

SENTENCE HOLES ARE FOR THE BIRDS

Write the New Words that best complete the sentences.

NEW WORDS
- directions
- gulps
- speckled
- narrow
- cliffs
- swiftly
- lizard
- glides
- ditches
- skinny

1. The long, _____ snake slithered through the small opening.
2. I saw that it was _____ with many bright colors.
3. A large, greedy _____ ate the insect.
4. It _____ it down greedily.
5. The road was so _____ that two cars could hardly fit on it.
6. The _____ on the side of the road were very deep.
7. An eagle _____ gracefully in the wind.
8. The eagle can also fly _____ to catch a small animal.
9. The wind blew in different _____ throughout the day.
10. The cabin was located high up on the _____.

SYNONYMS AND ANTONYMS ARE OPPOSITES

☞ **Synonyms** are words with nearly the same meaning. **Antonyms** are words that have opposite meanings.

huge and **large** are synonyms

thin and **fat** are antonyms

Write on the lines a synonym and an antonym for each word.

Synonyms
- alike
- huge
- thin
- swiftly
- rich
- healthy

	Synonyms	Antonyms
1. large	_____	_____
2. skinny	_____	_____
3. wealthy	_____	_____
4. well	_____	_____
5. same	_____	_____
6. quickly	_____	_____

Antonyms
- slowly
- fat
- different
- small
- sick
- poor

WORDS OF A FEATHER GROUP TOGETHER

☞ Groups of words that go together form **categories**. For example, **spoon**, **fork**, and **knife** belong to the category things you use to eat.

Read each category and circle the three words that belong in it.

1. things that glide
   birds   planes   skaters   rabbits

2. parts of a lizard
   fins   tail   body   head

3. things you gulp
   juice   milk   toothpaste   food

4. things that can be speckled
   eggs   walls   paintings   spoons

5. things that are swift
   rabbit   turtle   cheetah   horse

COMPARISONS ARE FOR THE BIRDS

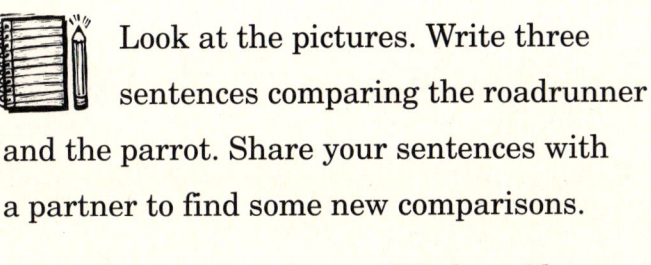

Look at the pictures. Write three sentences comparing the roadrunner and the parrot. Share your sentences with a partner to find some new comparisons.

The following questions will help guide you.

- What do you see covering each bird?
- What is different about each bird's head?
- How else are the birds different?

Use three New Words in your sentences.

DON'T BE A BIRD BRAIN

READ:
- *State Birds* by Elaine Landau. (Watts, 1992)
- *Bird of Prey* by Mary Hoffman. (Raintree, 1987)

STRANGE BUT TRUE BIRD FACTS

The roadrunner is the state bird of New Mexico.

The roadrunner is also called lizard bird, war bird, and running cuckoo.

The roadrunner can run as fast as 20 mph.

Kick up some dust! Take the test!

IMPROVE YOUR SCORE

Look over your test a last time to make sure you did not miss any questions and that your answers can be easily read by the teacher.

Complete each sentence with the best word or group of words. Fill in the circle for the answer at the bottom of the page.

1 Work that is done quickly is done . . . .
- A skinny
- B narrow
- C swiftly
- D slowly

2 Long, narrow holes in the earth are called . . . .
- A cliffs
- B directions
- C skinny
- D ditches

3 A dog with small marks all over its coat is . . . .
- A speckled
- B spoiled
- C skinny
- D narrow

4 A person who swallows something in a hurry . . .
- A chews it
- B bites it
- C gulps it
- D nibbles it

5 One kind of reptile is a . . . .
- A bird
- B lizard
- C roadrunner
- D gorilla

6 High and steep faces of rock and earth are called . . . .
- A ditches
- B hills
- C cliffs
- D deserts

Read each set of sentences. Select the answer that best completes the second sentence in the set. Fill in the circle for the answer at the bottom of the page.

7 The bird landed on a narrow patch of grass. Narrow means—
- A wide
- B long
- C small in width
- D short

8 Watch the plane as it glides through the sky. Glides means—
- A moves with difficulty
- B moves easily
- C moves slowly
- D moves quickly

9 The soldiers kept changing directions as they practiced marching. Directions means—
- A information
- B uniforms
- C shoes
- D routes

10 The roadrunner is a skinny bird. Skinny means—
- A fast
- B thin
- C small
- D fat

11 He did his work swiftly and went out to play. Swiftly means—
- A sloppily
- B fast
- C quietly
- D well

12 The ditches were filled with water after the heavy rain. Ditches means—
- A holes
- B cliffs
- C skies
- D clouds

ANSWERS

1 Ⓐ Ⓑ Ⓒ Ⓓ	4 Ⓐ Ⓑ Ⓒ Ⓓ	7 Ⓐ Ⓑ Ⓒ Ⓓ	10 Ⓐ Ⓑ Ⓒ Ⓓ
2 Ⓐ Ⓑ Ⓒ Ⓓ	5 Ⓐ Ⓑ Ⓒ Ⓓ	8 Ⓐ Ⓑ Ⓒ Ⓓ	11 Ⓐ Ⓑ Ⓒ Ⓓ
3 Ⓐ Ⓑ Ⓒ Ⓓ	6 Ⓐ Ⓑ Ⓒ Ⓓ	9 Ⓐ Ⓑ Ⓒ Ⓓ	12 Ⓐ Ⓑ Ⓒ Ⓓ

KILLER STORM HITS!
HURRICANE FLIERS HELP THOUSANDS

A **hurricane** is heading toward land with winds of almost two hundred miles per hour. Hurricane fliers, a crew of pilots and scientists, **board** a huge Lockheed Orion airplane. They fly into the hurricane to find out when and where the storm will hit land.

As the plane nears the giant storm, a **clap** of **thunder** is felt—then a blinding flash of light. The crew is calm, though. Then without warning, the plane suddenly drops two hundred feet. It has hit a **downward current** of air.

These scientists need **stamina** as they measure the air pressure, wind speed, temperature, and other information about the storm. Finally, the scientists report their **findings** to the National Oceanic and Atmospheric Administration. The NOAA warns people in the hurricane's **path**. They can board up their houses and leave the area to **avoid** the terrible storm.

"The lightning bolt shocked us all," says pilot.

CAUSE FOUND IN HIGH-FLYING STORY

What might be the main cause of this headline's appearance in a newspaper? **"Millions of People Flee Hurricane"**

Check the best answer

○ warnings by the NOAA

○ the crash of a Lockheed Orion airplane

○ hurricane flyers boarding their plane

○ thunder and lightning

Technology 83

ALPHABET AVOIDS DISORDER

☞ In a dictionary, **guide words** at the top of the page show the first and last entries on the page. All other entries on the page are in alphabetical order between these guide words.

Write the New Words in alphabetical order under the correct guide words.

NEW WORDS
hurricane
stamina
board
clap
thunder
downward
current
findings
path
avoid

avenge/classic
_____
_____
_____

cull/drain
_____
_____

fin/husky
_____
_____

patch/tie
_____
_____

MATCH THESE WORDS WITH THE MEANINGS

Match each New Word with its meaning. Write the letter of the meaning on the line next to the word.

____ 1. hurricane   a. noise in an electrical storm caused by moving masses of air
____ 2. stamina   b. information gathered by observing
____ 3. board   c. a tropical storm with violent winds
____ 4. clap   d. to keep out of the way of
____ 5. thunder   e. the strength to carry on
____ 6. downward   f. flow of water or wind
____ 7. current   g. track or trail
____ 8. findings   h. from higher to lower
____ 9. path   i. sudden loud noise
____ 10. avoid   j. to enter a vehicle

ANTONYMS ARE WORDS THAT ARE DIFFERENT

Antonyms are words that have opposite meanings.

black and **white**

near and **far**

WORD LIST
under
alive
south
freeze
war
wrong

Use words from the Word List to complete each antonym puzzle.

1. PEACE
2. DEAD
3. CORRECT
4. DEFROST
5. NORTH
6. OVER

WORDS BLOW IN TO FILL SENTENCE HOLES

Write the New Word that best completes each sentence.

1. The glider rode on a _____ of air.
2. They _____ swimming during an electrical storm.
3. I was frightened by the sudden _____ of thunder.
4. The winds of the _____ died down when the eye of the storm passed over us.
5. The plane hit a _____ current of wind.
6. The _____ of the hurricane flyers save many lives each year.
7. Driving a race car for many hours requires a lot of _____ .
8. The driver asked us to _____ the bus early.
9. The scientists were not sure what _____ the storm would take.
10. Lightning is dangerous; _____ is not.

PICTURE THAT!

NEW WORDS
- hurricane
- board
- thunder
- downward
- current
- findings
- path
- avoid

Write the New Word that best matches each picture.

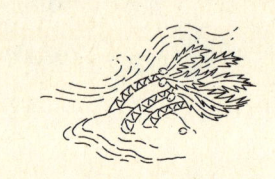

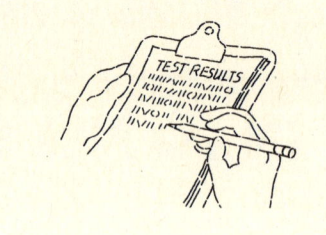

1. _____
2. _____
3. _____
4. _____
5. _____
6. _____
7. _____
8. _____

CAN YOU TOP THIS?

You may never have been in a hurricane, but chances are you can remember a bad storm of some kind. Write a story about it.

These questions will help you get started:
- What was the worst storm that you can remember?
- What did you do during the storm?
- What was it like after the storm was over?

Use at least three of the New Words in your story.

Fly on over to the test!

WEATHER BULLETIN

A *hurricane watch* means conditions are right for a hurricane. A *hurricane warning* means a hurricane has been sighted. Take cover!

EYE IN THE SKY

NOAA also tracks hurricanes using orbiting satellites with cameras in space.

WHAT TO KNOW BEFORE WINDS BLOW! READ:

- *Disastrous Hurricanes and Tornadoes* by Max and Charlotte Alth. (Watts, 1981)
- *Hurricane! The Rage of Hurricane Andrew.* (Gareth Stevens, 1993)

SECRETS TO SUCCESS ON TESTS

When looking for a word that means the same as another, replace the given word with your choice to see if it makes sense.

Read each group of words. Select the word or words that mean the <u>same</u> as the underlined word. Fill in the circle for the answer at the bottom of the page.

1   eye of a <u>hurricane</u>

    A   very strong wind storm
    B   heavy snowstorm
    C   ugly monster
    D   someone in a hurry

2   <u>thunder</u> and lightning

    A   strong wind
    B   streak of electricity
    C   heavy rain
    D   loud noise in an electrical storm

3   <u>downward</u> movement

    A   from lower to higher
    B   from higher to lower
    C   windy
    D   strong

4   report the <u>findings</u>

    A   lost things
    B   facts
    C   crimes
    D   bad storms

5   followed the <u>path</u>

    A   track
    B   leader
    C   flag
    D   call

6   tried to <u>avoid</u>

    A   meet with
    B   get near
    C   keep away from
    D   talk to

7   <u>stamina</u> to carry on

    A   feat
    B   share
    C   stick
    D   strength

8   <u>clap</u> of thunder

    A   whisper
    B   sudden loud sound
    C   rain storm
    D   blow

Read each sentence. Select the answer that best completes each one. Fill in the circle for the answer at the bottom of the page.

9   The athlete worked to increase his ____ before the long race.

    A   range   **C**   movement
    B   findings   **D**   stamina

10   I heard a ____ of thunder.

    A   storm   **C**   clap
    B   lightning   **D**   rain

11   We ____ our plane in a few minutes.

    A   arrive   **C**   avoid
    B   board   **D**   seat

12   The bird rode a ____ of wind.

    A   blow   **C**   findings
    B   current   **D**   blast

ANSWERS

1	Ⓐ Ⓑ Ⓒ Ⓓ	4	Ⓐ Ⓑ Ⓒ Ⓓ	7	Ⓐ Ⓑ Ⓒ Ⓓ	10	Ⓐ Ⓑ Ⓒ Ⓓ
2	Ⓐ Ⓑ Ⓒ Ⓓ	5	Ⓐ Ⓑ Ⓒ Ⓓ	8	Ⓐ Ⓑ Ⓒ Ⓓ	11	Ⓐ Ⓑ Ⓒ Ⓓ
3	Ⓐ Ⓑ Ⓒ Ⓓ	6	Ⓐ Ⓑ Ⓒ Ⓓ	9	Ⓐ Ⓑ Ⓒ Ⓓ	12	Ⓐ Ⓑ Ⓒ Ⓓ

BACK TO THE FUTURE

A horse **trots** down a dirt road pulling a **buggy**. Inside, a bearded man is dressed in **denim** overalls without the **convenience** of zippers. His wife wears a **bonnet** and **shawl**. Suddenly a car zooms past the buggy. For a split second, the past meets the future.

This is a daily experience for the Amish, or "plain" people. The Amish first came to Pennsylvania from Europe seeking religious freedom. Today they still focus their actions and **lifestyle** on religious **principles**. For example, they **discipline** themselves to do without things such as TV that do not fit in with their religious principles.

Just what do the Amish do for fun, anyway? On winter afternoons you might find Amish children with skis in hand. The children attach ropes to the horse's **harness**. One child jumps on the horse's back while the others slip into their skis. The skiers grab onto the rope, and with a kick they're off. They race through the barnyard, over snowdrifts, and down the road. These skiers may make the Olympics look rather tame.

READERS WONDER ABOUT CAUSE

Why do most of the Amish not watch TV?

Check the best answer.

❏ They are too poor to buy a TV.

❏ They are too busy playing in the snow.

❏ They ride in their buggies instead.

❏ TV does not fit in with their religious principles.

88 Heritage

HARNESS THIS ABC LIST

Guide words at the top of the page in a dictionary show the first and last entries on the page. All other entries on the page are in alphabetical order between the guide words.

Write the New Words in alphabetical order under the correct guide words.

NEW WORDS

trots	denim	bonnet	lifestyle	discipline
buggy	convenience	shawl	principles	harness

avenge/classic
_____
_____

control/dispose
_____
_____
_____

harmful/lighten
_____
_____

pretzel/true
_____
_____
_____

WORDS AND MEANINGS MATCH

Match each New Word with its meaning. Write the letter of the meaning on the line next to the word.

____ 1. trots   a. the straps that attach a horse to a buggy
____ 2. buggy   b. a hat for women and girls that ties under the chin
____ 3. denim   c. thing that makes life easier
____ 4. convenience   d. to limit or to force one to do something
____ 5. bonnet   e. a horse-drawn vehicle
____ 6. shawl   f. tough blue material used in work and play clothes
____ 7. lifestyle   g. a type of scarf worn over the shoulders
____ 8. principles   h. steps along quickly
____ 9. discipline   i. the way people live
____ 10. harness   j. rules by which a person acts

HARD-WORKING WORDS COMPLETE THE JOB

Write the New Word that best completes each sentence.

1. I live by the same _____ as my parents do.
2. The Amish woman used a _____ to keep herself warm.
3. You will want to _____ yourself not to eat the candy.
4. The horse _____ down the road ahead of all the cars.
5. The Amish farmer used a _____ to take his family to town.
6. Sturdy _____ clothes last a long time.
7. Some Amish people do not have the _____ of electricity.
8. Your _____ is very different from mine.
9. Does that horse like to be in its _____ ?
10. The _____ kept the sun off my face.

NEW WORDS
trots
buggy
denim
convenience
bonnet
shawl
lifestyle
principles
discipline
harness

MULTIPLE MEANINGS CAN SPELL TROUBLE

Many words have more than one meaning. **Context clues** in sentences can help you determine the meanings of these words.

Bat can mean an animal or a wooden club used in baseball.

The words drill and chest each have more than one meaning. Write the number of the best meaning on the line next to each sentence.

chest
a. a heavy box with a lid
b. a piece of furniture with drawers
c. the upper part of the body

drill
a. a tool with a sharp point
b. a practice of something over and over

____ 1. I opened the drawer and put my clothes in the chest next to my bed.
____ 2. Dad went to work even though he has a bad chest cold.
____ 3. Mother has a small jewelry chest for her rings and necklaces.
____ 4. Every day our teacher has a drill on multiplication facts.
____ 5. The carpenter has an electric drill that he uses to make holes.

SECRET ANSWER REVEALED

Answer the following question by writing the New Words on the lines next to the clues.

What event do Amish people hold to help another member of their community?

1. a hat for women and girls   __ __ __ __ __ __ __
2. a scarf worn on the shoulders   __ __ __ __ __
3. steps along quickly   __ __ __ __ __
4. thing that makes life easier   __ __ __ __ __ __ __ __ __
5. rules by which people act   __ __ __ __ __ __
6. straps that attach a horse to a buggy __ __ __ __ __ __ __
7. the way people live   __ __ __ __ __ __ __ __
8. to limit or to force one to do something __ __ __ __ __ __ __
9. a device to fasten two edges of material   Z I P P E R
10. tough blue material used to make clothes __ __ __ __
11. a horse-drawn vehicle   __ __ __ __ __

SOMEONE I'LL NEVER FORGET

Who is the most unusual person you have ever met? Write a description of this person. Share your description with a friend.

Use these questions to help you get started:
- Why is this person so unusual?
- How does this person look?
- How does this person act?

Use at least three of the New Words in your description.

TRADITION! WHAT DOES IT MEAN TO BE AMISH?

✻ Amish children only go to school through the eighth grade. Each boy learns his father's trade, and each girl learns housekeeping skills from her mother.

✻ Amish children are raised using two languages. Their first language is German, and their second is English.

HOW DO THEY DO THAT? READ:

- *Tales from Peoli Road* by Eli Beachy. (Herald Press, 1992)
- *Amish Roots* by John Hostetler. (The Johns Hopkins University Press, 1989)

Trot over to the test!

SECRETS TO SUCCESS ON TESTS

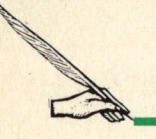

If you have time at the end of a test, reread the directions and test questions.

Complete each definition with the best word or phrase. Fill in the circle for the answer at the bottom of the page.

1. A <u>bonnet</u> is a—
   - A girl's blouse
   - B woman's hat
   - C coat
   - D shoe

2. To <u>discipline</u> is to—
   - A limit
   - B show
   - C hear
   - D see

3. A <u>convenience</u> is something—
   - A useless
   - B to sell
   - C to buy
   - D useful

4. A <u>shawl</u> may act as a—
   - A coat
   - B hat
   - C shoe
   - D shirt

5. <u>Principles</u> are—
   - A leaders
   - B teachers
   - C rules
   - D sums

6. A <u>lifestyle</u> is a—
   - A kind of jacket
   - B way someone lives
   - C way to talk
   - D kind of look

Read each sentence. Select the answer that best completes each one. Fill in the circle for the answer at the bottom of the page.

7. Many Amish use a ____ to get around.
   - A denim
   - B convenience
   - C shawl
   - D buggy

8. The horse ____ down the road.
   - A pants
   - B trots
   - C harness
   - D bonnet

9. The worker wore ____ overalls.
   - A shawl
   - B denim
   - C harness
   - D bonnet

10. I attached the ____ to the horse.
    - A harness
    - B denim
    - C convenience
    - D principles

11. The ____ of the Amish may be different from yours.
    - A convenience
    - B harness
    - C lifestyle
    - D buggy

12. Our teacher is trying to ____ us so we will be better students.
    - A trot
    - B denim
    - C shawl
    - D discipline

ANSWERS

1 Ⓐ Ⓑ Ⓒ Ⓓ	4 Ⓐ Ⓑ Ⓒ Ⓓ	7 Ⓐ Ⓑ Ⓒ Ⓓ	10 Ⓐ Ⓑ Ⓒ Ⓓ
2 Ⓐ Ⓑ Ⓒ Ⓓ	5 Ⓐ Ⓑ Ⓒ Ⓓ	8 Ⓐ Ⓑ Ⓒ Ⓓ	11 Ⓐ Ⓑ Ⓒ Ⓓ
3 Ⓐ Ⓑ Ⓒ Ⓓ	6 Ⓐ Ⓑ Ⓒ Ⓓ	9 Ⓐ Ⓑ Ⓒ Ⓓ	12 Ⓐ Ⓑ Ⓒ Ⓓ

MIND BOGGLING MOVIES
CARTOONS FLASH 24 PICTURES EVERY SECOND

Have you ever wondered how **cartoons** are made? Look at this picture showing a piece of **film**. Each frame has a picture that looks very much like the others around it. Each one shows just a tiny bit of **movement**.

Cartoonists **understand** how to use this idea to make drawings into movies. First, they draw **scenery** for each part of the story. Then they draw people and animals. They must draw twenty-four pictures for each second of the show. Each picture is only a little different from the one before it. It takes **thousands** of these drawings to make one story.

Each picture is then colored, and the pictures are put on film. A **special** type of **camera** is used. These pictures are flashed on a **screen** one after the other. The people and animals seem to be moving. Real people talk for the people and animals in the drawings. The actors' and actresses' voices are added to the film.

Now the drawings seem almost real. As you can see, a great **deal** of work goes into the cartoons that you enjoy watching!

SEARCH FOR THE ANSWERS STILL ON

What happens when pictures with only small changes are shown one after another?

Check the best answer.

○ They seems to talk. ○ They become real.

○ They seem to move. ○ People work hard.

Entertainment 93

NEW WORDS FRAMED! GUIDE WORDS BLAMED!

👉 In the dictionary, **guide words** at the top of the page show the first and last entries on the page. All other entries on the page are in alphabetical order between those words.

Write the New Words in alphabetical order under the correct guide words.

calm/dear	death/mow	much/speed	spend/undo
_____	_____	_____	_____
_____	_____	_____	_____
_____		_____	

New Words
- understand
- cartoons
- film
- movement
- scenery
- thousands
- special
- camera
- screen
- deal

WORDS AND MEANINGS ALL MATCH UP!

Match each New Word below with its meaning. Write the letter of the meaning on the line next to the word.

____ 1. screen
____ 2. special
____ 3. film
____ 4. scenery
____ 5. understand
____ 6. cartoons
____ 7. deal
____ 8. thousands
____ 9. movement
____ 10. camera

a. motion pictures made of humorous drawings
b. more than one thousand
c. to get the meaning of; know what is meant by something or someone
d. a thin, flexible material on which a series of pictures, as for a movie, appear
e. a surface on which movies or television pictures are shown
f. the background objects in a movie or play; the way a certain area looks
g. the act of moving or a way of moving
h. a closed box for taking pictures
i. not like others; different; distinct
j. a large amount; very much

COMPLETED SENTENCES GIVE BIG PICTURE!

Write the New Words that best complete the sentences.

1. We thought the snake was alive, but it made no _____ .
2. Our family enjoyed the _____ as we drove along the ocean.
3. There were _____ of people at the fair this weekend.
4. I did not _____ the question, so Mrs. Davis helped me.
5. Every Saturday morning, I watch _____ on television.
6. Did you remember to load the _____ in the camera?
7. Grandpa bought a TV with a large _____ .
8. This _____ takes clear photographs.
9. Mrs. Thomas likes the boat a great _____ more than the car.
10. We usually make birthdays _____ by having a party.

SUFFIXES CHANGE MEANING

A **suffix** is a word part that can be added to the end of a root word. Adding a suffix changes the meaning of a root word. For example, the suffix **able** means <u>able to</u> or <u>able to be</u>.

Root Word   Suffix   New Word
work   +   **able**   =   **workable**

Complete each sentence by adding the suffix <u>able</u> to the word.

1. She speaks so softly that her words are not _____ .
   (understand)
2. I do not know if this material is _____ or not.
   (wash)
3. This is the most _____ book I have ever read.
   (enjoy)
4. The roads were not _____ during the winter storm.
   (pass)
5. Is the mower still _____ , or does it need repair?
   (use)
6. My answer was not _____ .
   (accept)

BRAINSTORM CAPTURED ON FILM

What comes to your mind as you think about each heading below? Quickly make a list of as many ideas as you can think of. When you are finished, go back and review what you have written.

Write down as many words or phrases as you can think of under each heading.

things <u>special</u> to you
_____
_____
_____

some <u>cartoon</u> shows
_____
_____
_____

places where you would want to have a <u>camera</u>
_____
_____
_____

things you think are hard to <u>understand</u>
_____
_____
_____

what there are <u>thousands</u> of
_____
_____
_____

\>\> Fast forward to the test!

CREATE SOME LAUGHS ON YOUR OWN

Read these books:
- *Cartooning* by Anthony Hodge. (Gloucester Press, 1992)
- *Cartooning for Kids* by Carol Benjamin. (Thomas Crowell, 1982)

NEW CARTOON STRIP TELLS ALL

Think about a day when something funny happened to you. Draw a cartoon strip and write a script to go with it.

Think about these questions as you write.
- Where were you?
- Who was with you?
- What happened?

Use at least three New Words in your script.

CAN YOU GUESS?

How many drawings does it take to make one minute of an animated cartoon?

Answer: Approximately 1,440 drawings.

TEST-TAKING SECRETS REVEALED

It helps to have a quiet room in which to take a test. Do your part in keeping the room quiet.

Read each group of words. Select the answer that means the <u>same</u> as the underlined word. Fill in the circle for the answer at the bottom of the page.

1 saw the <u>film</u>
   - A scrapbook
   - B page
   - C movie
   - D book

2 a sudden <u>movement</u>
   - A sound
   - B action
   - C feeling
   - D sight

3 painted the <u>scenery</u>
   - A background objects
   - B colorful walls
   - C stage area
   - D people and animals

4 <u>thousands</u> of dollars
   - A more than one hundred
   - B more than one thousand
   - C numbers
   - D millions

5 a <u>special</u> gift
   - A different
   - B wrapped
   - C birthday
   - D expensive

6 a great <u>deal</u> of time
   - A box
   - B amount
   - C size
   - D width

Read the paragraphs. Select the words that best fit in the blanks. Fill in the circles for the answers at the bottom of the page.

I like to watch __7__ on Saturday mornings. I'm reading a book on how a __8__ is made. Now I __9__ what a big job it is to make my favorite cartoon, Mickey Mouse.

7 A screen
   B cartoons
   C movement
   D camera

8 A form
   B screen
   C deal
   D film

9 A understand
   B wonder
   C think
   D talk about

The pictures I took with my new __10__ were flashed on the __11__ for all to see. I watched the reactions of the audience with a great __12__ of pride.

10 A screen
   B camera
   C film
   D cartoons

11 A camera
   B film
   C screen
   D cartoons

12 A movement
   B deal
   C special
   D scenery

Young At Heart

Have you met Henry Huggins or Ramona Quimby? Henry and Ramona are sure to make you laugh. You won't meet them playing in your **neighborhood**, however. Henry and Ramona are **characters** in books written by Beverly Cleary.

Even though Beverly had **difficulty** learning to read, she loved books. Beverly learned to read when she was eight. After that, she read almost every children's book in her town's library. However, the characters in the books were not **similar** to Beverly. It seemed as though they were always very **wealthy** or very poor. Many of them were from **foreign** lands. Beverly wanted to read **humorous** stories about **ordinary** children like herself.

When Beverly finished college, she became a children's librarian. Soon she began to write the stories she enjoyed telling. Many of her ideas came from **experiences** she had while growing up in a **rural** town in Oregon. She also got ideas from the experiences of people around her. When you read about the adventures of Henry Huggins and Ramona Quimby, you will get to know the young Beverly Cleary and her friends, too!

THIS GROWN-UP WRITES BOOKS FOR CHILDREN

SEARCH FOR THE DETAILS

Why did Beverly Cleary create her own characters
Check the best answer.
○ She wanted children to read about ordinary children like themselves.
○ She wanted to be a librarian.
○ She wanted to be very wealthy
○ She wanted to read about her own life as a writer.

THE AMAZING ALPHABET

☞ In the dictionary, **guide words** at the top of the page show the first and last entries on the page. All other entries on the page are in alphabetical order between those words.

Write the New Words in alphabetical order under the correct guide words.

champion/explode
_____
_____
_____

express/hump
_____
_____

hurry/rust
_____
_____
_____

shock/weather
_____
_____

New Words

ordinary   neighborhood   similar
difficulty   humorous   experiences
foreign   wealthy   rural
characters

WORDS AND MEANINGS - MATCH THEM UP

Match each New Word below with its meaning. Write the letter of the meaning on the line next to the word.

____ 1. difficulty
____ 2. similar
____ 3. foreign
____ 4. wealthy
____ 5. characters
____ 6. ordinary
____ 7. experiences
____ 8. humorous
____ 9. rural
____ 10. neighborhood

a. usual; regular; normal
b. having to do with land around farms
c. trouble or the cause of trouble
d. a small part or district of a city or town
e. almost but not exactly the same; alike
f. persons in a story or a play
g. funny or amusing; comical
h. things that one has done or lived through
i. that which is outside one's country or region
j. having wealth; rich

INCOMPLETE SENTENCES NEED YOUR HELP

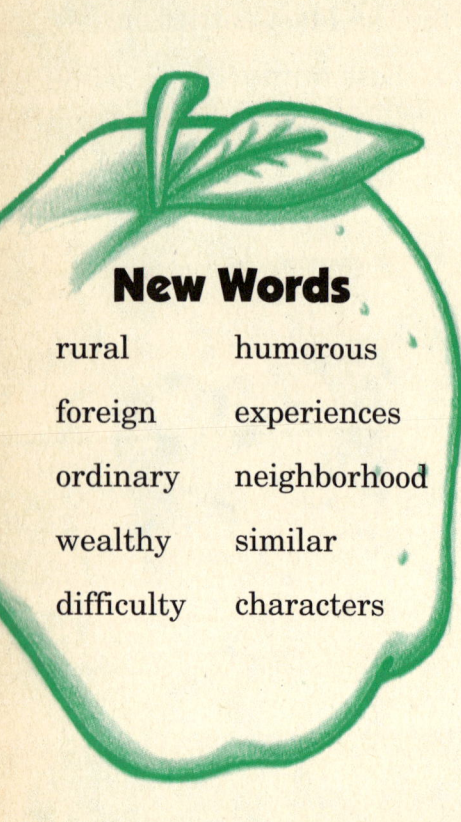

Write the New Words that best complete the sentences.

My family lives in a _____ town. There aren't many children in my _____ , so I spend many hours reading. I love reading! Sometimes I have _____ understanding all the words. There are words that look so _____ I can't tell them apart. Books about _____ lands are very interesting. If I were _____ , I would travel to many of those far-away countries. I also like to read books with animals as the main _____ . These _____ books usually make me laugh out loud. My favorite book, however, is about an _____ boy who is my age. I was surprised to read how he had many of the same _____ at school that I have had.

New Words

rural	humorous
foreign	experiences
ordinary	neighborhood
wealthy	similar
difficulty	characters

WORDS DIVIDED OVER SYLLABLES

Words can be divided into smaller word parts or **syllables**. For example, say the word <u>understand</u> and listen for its syllables.

un   der   stand

Say each New Word and listen for the syllables. Write the words leaving a space between syllables. Use the dictionary if you are not sure where to divide a word.

1. ordinary _____
2. wealthy _____
3. rural _____
4. experiences _____
5. foreign _____

6. difficulty _____
7. neighborhood _____
8. humorous _____
9. similar _____
10. characters _____

ANALOGIES ARE EVERYWHERE

☞ **Analogies** show us the relationships between things.
mouse is to **animal** as **rose** is to **flower**

Complete the following analogies using some of the New Words.

1. _____ are to books as actors are to movies

2. poor is to needy as rich is to _____

3. common is to _____ as unusual is to strange

4. _____ is to city as county is to state

5. _____ is to laugh as sad is to cry

6. farm is to _____ as skyscraper is to urban

Readers Rave Over Favorite Writers!
SURVEY SHOWS MOST POPULAR AUTHORS

Who is your favorite author? Go to the library and find some information about that author. You might ask the librarian for help. Write a short report about the author.

The following questions will help you get started.
- What books has the author written?
- What is your favorite book by this author and why?
- Is there anything interesting about the author's life?

Use at least three New Words in your report.

You're right! It's time for the test.

WANT TO KNOW MORE ABOUT BEVERLY CLEARY?
Check out these videos...
- *Mouse and the Motorcycle* by Beverly Cleary. (Strand VCI Entertainment, 1991)
- *Ramona Goodbye* by Beverly Cleary. (Atlantis Films, Ltd., 1989)

...And books!
- *Something About the Author* by Anne Commire. (Gale Research Company, 1986)
- *Ramona Forever* by Beverly Cleary. (Dell Publishing Company, 1984)

SHOCKING BUT TRUE!
In first grade, Beverly Cleary was in the Blackbirds reading group. She hated reading and those other Blackbirds! She was the only girl in that group.

A SHARP FACT!
Beverly Cleary's husband brought her home a pencil sharpener. She found some paper in her linen closet and decided to write a book.

SCORE HIGHER ON TESTS

When you are finished, go back and check that you marked your answers on the correct lines in the answer box.

Read each group of words. Select the answer that means the <u>opposite</u> of the underlined word. Fill in the circle for the answer at the bottom of the page.

1. a <u>rural</u> area
   - A business
   - B farming
   - C parking
   - D city

2. a <u>wealthy</u> uncle
   - A sick
   - B poor
   - C rich
   - D elderly

3. an <u>ordinary</u> day
   - A sunny
   - B regular
   - C beautiful
   - D unusual

4. walked with <u>difficulty</u>
   - A ease
   - B trouble
   - C help
   - D sadness

5. a <u>similar</u> dress
   - A alike
   - B different
   - C unusual
   - D usual

6. a <u>humorous</u> story
   - A long
   - B funny
   - C short
   - D serious

Read each set of sentences. Select the word that completes the first sentence according to the stated meaning. Fill in the circle for the answer at the bottom of the page.

7. The police officer is the best-liked person in our ____. Which word indicates an area of homes and businesses?
   - A school
   - B business
   - C neighborhood
   - D country

8. The ____ in the play were Henry Huggins and his friends. Which word indicates the parts or roles in the play?
   - A characters
   - B experiences
   - C actors
   - D writers

9. From which ____ land did Columbus come? Which word indicates the land was some other than the one the speaker lives in?
   - A warm
   - B rich
   - C poor
   - D foreign

10. The ____ we had this year in school will be happy memories all summer long. Which word indicates events that are lived through?
    - A characters
    - B experiences
    - C results
    - D vacations

11. We enjoyed a ride through the ____ area outside of town. Which word indicates that the area was a farming district?
    - A town
    - B suburb
    - C urban
    - D rural

12. One of his goals is to become ____ some day. Which word indicates that one of his goals was to have a lot of money?
    - A rural
    - B wealthy
    - C humorous
    - D ordinary

ANSWERS

1 Ⓐ Ⓑ Ⓒ Ⓓ	4 Ⓐ Ⓑ Ⓒ Ⓓ	7 Ⓐ Ⓑ Ⓒ Ⓓ	10 Ⓐ Ⓑ Ⓒ Ⓓ
2 Ⓐ Ⓑ Ⓒ Ⓓ	5 Ⓐ Ⓑ Ⓒ Ⓓ	8 Ⓐ Ⓑ Ⓒ Ⓓ	11 Ⓐ Ⓑ Ⓒ Ⓓ
3 Ⓐ Ⓑ Ⓒ Ⓓ	6 Ⓐ Ⓑ Ⓒ Ⓓ	9 Ⓐ Ⓑ Ⓒ Ⓓ	12 Ⓐ Ⓑ Ⓒ Ⓓ

Pronunciation Key

Letters	Show the Sound of	Written as
a	c<u>a</u>t	KAT
ah	<u>o</u>dd	AHD
ahr	b<u>a</u>r	BAHR
aw	l<u>aw</u>n	LAWN
ay	p<u>ay</u>	PAY
b	<u>b</u>ib	BIB
ch	<u>ch</u>ip	CHIP
d	<u>d</u>eed	DEED
e	p<u>e</u>t	PET
ee	b<u>ee</u>	BEE
er	c<u>are</u>	KER
eye	<u>i</u>sland	EYE luhnd
f	<u>f</u>ast	FAST
g	<u>g</u>ag	GAG
h	<u>h</u>at	HAT
i	p<u>i</u>t	PIT
ir	d<u>ear</u>	DIR
j	<u>j</u>oke	JOHK
k	<u>k</u>it	KIT
l	<u>l</u>id	LID
m	<u>m</u>an	MAN
n	<u>n</u>o	NOH
ng	thi<u>ng</u>	THING
oh	g<u>o</u>	GOH
oo	m<u>oo</u>n	MOON
or	st<u>ore</u>	STOR
ow	<u>ou</u>t	OWT
oy	j<u>oy</u>	JOY
p	<u>p</u>op	PAHP
r	<u>r</u>at	RAT
s	<u>s</u>ee	SEE
sh	<u>sh</u>ip	SHIP
t	<u>t</u>in	TIN
th	<u>th</u>ing	THING
th	<u>th</u>en	THEN
u	b<u>oo</u>k	BUK
uh	c<u>u</u>t	KUHT
ur	h<u>er</u>	HUR
v	<u>v</u>ase	VAYS
w	<u>w</u>ith	WITH
y	<u>y</u>et	YET
z	<u>z</u>ebra	ZEE bruh
zh	vi<u>s</u>ion	VIZH uhn

GLOSSARY

A a

a•dults (ah DUHLTS) *n.* men or women who are fully grown up; mature people

ad•ver•tis•ing (AD ver teyez ing) *n.* public announcement of goods for sale

al•lowed (ah LOWD) *v.* let be done; permitted

al•though (ol THOH) *conj.* in spite of the fact; even; though

a•maz•ing (ah MAYZ ing) *adj.* causing great surprise or wonder

a•mount (ah MOWNT) *n.* a quantity

ar•e•a (ER ee ah) *n.* a part of the earth's surface; region

at•mos•phere (AT muhs fir) *n.* the air around the earth

at•tic (AT ik) *n.* room or space just below the roof of a house

au•to•mo•bile (AHT uh muh BEEL) *n.* a car; a vehicle moved by an engine that is part of it

a•void (ah VOYD) *v.* to keep out of the way of

B b

bal•ance (BAL ahns) *n.* the ability to keep one's body steady without falling; stability

bas•ket•ball (BAS ket bawl) *n.* organized game of shooting a ball through a hoop

bat•tle (BAT uhl) *n.* any fight or struggle; conflict

blind (BLEYEND) *adj.* not able to see; having no sight

block•ing (BLAHK ing) *n.* the act of trying to stop an opponent from scoring

board (BORD) *v.* to enter a vehicle

bon•net (BAHN et) *n.* a hat for women and girls that ties under the chin

born (BORN) *v.* brought into life or being

bor•rowed (BAHR ohd) *v.* used for awhile with the understanding one would return it later

bug•gy (BUHG ee) *n.* a horse-drawn vehicle

busi•ness (BIZ nes) *n.* a commercial establishment such as a store; one's work or occupation

C c

cab•in (KAB in) *n.* a small house built in a simple, rough way, usually of wood

103

cam•er•a (KAM er ah) *n.* a closed box for taking pictures

cap•sules (KAP suhlz) *n.* small containers

car•ry (KER ee) *v.* to take from one place to another; to transport or conduct

car•toons (kahr TOONZ) *n.* motion pictures made of humorous drawings

cause (KAWZ) *v.* to make happen; bring about

cells (SELZ) *n.* very tiny units of living matter

char•ac•ters (KER ahk terz) *n.* persons in a story or a play

clap (KLAP) *n.* sudden loud noise

cliffs (KLIFS) *n.* high steep faces of rock that go down sharply with little or no slope

coin (KOYN) *n.* a piece of metal money having a certain value

combed (KOHMBD) *v.* smoothed, arranged, or cleaned with a comb

com•mon (KAHM en) *adj.* of the usual kind; ordinary

com•mu•ni•cate (kuh MYOO ni kayt) *v.* to pass on information

con•tract (kahn TRAKT) *v.* to tighten or become smaller

con•ven•ience (kuhn VEEN yens) *n.* thing that makes life easier

cough (KOF) *v.* to force air out of the throat

cour•age (KUR ij) *n.* bravery

court (KORT) *n.* the area on which a basketball game is played

crowd (KROWD) *v.* to come together in a large group

crutch (KRUHCH) *n.* anything that gives support or help; something that can be leaned on

cur•rent (KUR ent) *n.* flow of water or wind

D d

dam•aged (DAM ijd) *v.* injured or harmed in a way that results in a loss of health or value

deaf (DEF) *adj.* not able to hear or hardly able to hear

deal (DEEL) *n.* a large amount; very much

de•cid•ed (dee SEYED ed) *v.* chose after some thought; made up one's mind

den•im (DEN im) *n.* tough blue material used in work and play clothes

des•ert (DEZ ert) *n.* a dry, sandy region with little or no plant life

dif•fi•cul•ty (DIF i kuhl tee) *n.* trouble or the cause of trouble

dines (DEYENZ) *v.* eats a meal

di•rec•tions (de REK shuhnz) *n.* the points toward which things face, or the lines along which things move or lie

dis•as•ters (di ZAS terz) *n.* happenings that cause damage or suffering, as a flood or earthquake

dis•ci•pline (DIS i plin) *v.* to limit or to force one to do something

ditch•es (DICH ez) *n.* long, narrow openings dug in the earth; trenches

down•ward (DOWN werd) *adj.* from higher to lower

drifts (DRIFTS) *v.* is carried along by a current of water or air

dur•ing (DUR ing) *prep.* throughout the whole time of; all through

E e

en•ter (EN ter) *v.* to come or go in or into

ex•pect (ek SPEKT) *v.* to think that something will happen or come; look forward to

ex•per•i•enc•es (ek SPIR ee ens ez) *n.* things that one has done or lived through

F f

fe•male (FEE mayl) *adj.* of or for women or girls; of the group that is the mother of the offspring

film (FILM) *n.* a thin, flexible material on which a series of pictures, as for a movie, appear

find•ings (FEYEND ingz) *n.* information gathered by observing

fluf•fy (FLUHF ee) *adj.* soft and light

fol•li•cle (FAHL i kel) *n.* the sac in which a hair root sits

force (FORS) *v.* to make do something by using strength or power of some kind

for•eign (FOR in) *adj.* that which is outside one's country or region

for•est (FOR est) *n.* a thick growth of trees covering a large piece of land; large woods

form (FORM) *v.* to give a certain shape to

for•ward (FOR werd) *adv.* toward a point in front

fro•zen (FROH zen) *v.* turned into or covered with ice

G g

glides (GLEYEDZ) *v.* moves along in a smooth and easy way, as in skating

globe (GLOHB) *n.* the earth
go•ril•la (guh RIL uh) *n.* the largest and the strongest of the apes, found in Africa
greed•y (GREED ee) *adj.* wanting or taking all that one can get with no thought of what others need; selfish
grouch•y (GROW chee) *adj.* to be in a bad mood; cross and complaining
guard (GAHRD) *v.* to move so as to keep a player from scoring
gulps (GUHLPS) *v.* swallows in a hurried or greedy way

H h

hard•ly (HAHRD lee) *adv.* almost not; scarcely
har•ness (HAHR nes) *n.* the straps that attach a horse to a buggy
hatched (HACHD) *v.* to have brought forth young birds, fish, or turtles from eggs
his•to•ry (HIS tuhr ee) *n.* all the recorded events of the past
hon•est (AHN est) *adj.* truthful; capable of being trusted
hour•glass (OWR glas) *n.* a device for measuring time by the trickling of sand from one glass bulb through a small opening to another bulb below it
huge (HYOOJ) *adj.* very large; immense
hu•mor•ous (HYOO muhr uhs) *adj.* funny or amusing; comical
hur•ri•cane (HUR i kayn) *n.* a tropical storm with violent winds
hus•kies (HUS keez) *n.* strong dogs used for pulling sleds

I i

ice•bergs (EYES burgz) *n.* masses of ice broken off from a glacier and floating in the sea
in•su•la•tion (in suh LAY shuhn) *n.* a layer of material that protects
in•ter•est•ing (IN ter est ing) *adj.* stirring up one's interest; exciting
in•vol•un•tar•y (in VAH len ter ee) *adj.* automatic and uncontrolled

K k

kan•ga•roos (kang gah ROOZ) *n.* animals of Australia with short forelegs and strong, large hind legs, with which they make long leaps
knots (NAHTS) *n.* fastenings made by tying together parts or pieces of such things as string and rope

L l

lan•guage (LANG gwij) *n.* human speech or writing that stands for speech
leap (LEEP) *v.* to move oneself suddenly from the ground by using the leg muscles; jump; spring
life•style (LEYEF steyel) *n.* the way people live
liz•ard (LIZ erd) *n.* a reptile with a long, slender body and tail, scaly skin, and four legs

M m

mag•a•zines (mag ah ZEENZ) *n.* collections of writings that come out regularly
male (MAYL) *adj.* of or for men or boys; of the group that is the father of the offspring
mate (MAYT) *n.* one part of a pair
ma•te•ri•al (mah TER ee ahl) *n.* cloth or other fabric
melt (MELT) *v.* to change from a solid to a liquid by heat
mes•sag•es (MES ij ez) *n.* pieces of news, requests, facts, sent from one person to another
mind (MEYEND) *n.* the part of a person that thinks, reasons, feels, decides
mis•take (mi STAYK) *n.* an idea, answer, or act that is wrong; error or blunder
mod•ern (MAHD ern) *adj.* of the period in which you live
mois•ture (MOYS cher) *n.* fine drops of water in the air or on a surface; dampness
move•ment (MOOV ment) *n.* the act of moving or a way of moving
mush•ers (MUSH erz) *n.* dog sled drivers

N n

nar•row (NER oh) *adj.* small in width; less wide than usual

near•ly (NIR lee) *adv.* almost; not quite
neigh•bor•hood (NAY ber hud) *n.* a small part or district of a city or town
nor•mal (NOR mel) *adj.* agreeing with a standard or norm; natural; usual

O o

op•po•nents (ah POH nents) *n.* the players on the other team
or•di•nar•y (ORD uhn er ee) *adj.* usual; regular; normal

P p

past (PAST) *n.* the time that has gone by
path (PATH) *n.* track or trail
per•fumes (pur FYOOMZ) *n.* pleasant smells or fragrances
pill (PIL) *n.* a little ball or capsule of medicine to be swallowed whole
pokes (POHKS) *v.* pushes or jabs, as with a stick or finger
pos•si•ble (PAHS i bel) *adj.* capable of existing or happening
pouch (POWCH) *n.* a loose fold of skin, like a pocket, on the belly of certain female animals in which they carry their newborn young
pow•er•ful (POW er fuhl) *adj.* having much power; strong or influential
prai•rie (PRER ee) *n.* a large area of level or rolling, grassy land without many trees
pre•pares (pree PERZ) *v.* makes ready
pres•i•dent (PREZ i dent) *n.* the head of the United States government; the highest officer of a company, club, college, and so on
prin•ci•ples (PRIN si pelz) *n.* rules by which a person acts

Q q

quick (KWIK) *adj.* swift and speedy

R r

rac•ing (RAYS ing) *n.* the act of taking part in a contest of speed
re•bound•ing (ree BOWND ing) *n.* the act of catching a basketball as it bounces off the backboard or rim
re•ceived (ree SEEVD) *v.* to have taken or got what was given or sent
re•cent•ly (REE sent lee) *adv.* of a time just before now; lately
reins (RAYNZ) *n.* narrow strips of leather used to guide horses or dogs
rob•ber (RAHB ber) *n.* a person who steals by using force or threats
roots (ROOTS) *n.* the part of a plant that grows in the ground
ru•ral (RUR el) *adj.* having to do with land around farms

S s

scarce (SKERS) *adj.* not common; rarely seen
sce•ner•y (SEEN er ee) *n.* the background objects in a movie or play; the way a certain area looks
scent (SENT) *n.* odor or aroma
scratch (SKRACH) *v.* to scrape or rub
screen (SKREEN) *n.* a surface on which movies or television pictures are shown
search (SURCH) *v.* to try to find
set•tlers (SET lerz) *n.* people who go to live in a new country, colony, or region
sev•er•al (SEV er uhl) *adj.* more than two but not many; a few
sews (SOHZ) *v.* fastens or joins with stitches
shape (SHAYP) *n.* the way something looks because of its outline; outer form; figure
shawl (SHAWL) *n.* a type of scarf worn over the shoulders
shin•y (SHEYEN ee) *adj.* giving off light or reflecting light; bright
shiv•er•ing (SHIV er ing) *v.* shaking from cold or fear
shoot•ing (SHOOT ing) *n.* the act of trying to make a basket in the game of basketball
sim•i•lar (SIM i ler) *adj.* almost but not exactly the same; alike
skin (SKIN) *n.* outer covering of an animal's or a person's body
skin•ny (SKIN ee) *adj.* very lean or thin
some•times (SUM teyemz) *adv.* once in a while
sound (SOWND) *adj.* deep and undisturbed
space (SPAYS) *n.* the area that stretches in all directions, has no limits, and contains all things in the universe
spe•cial (SPESH el) *adj.* not like others; different; distinct
speck•led (SPEK uhld) *adj.* having small marks

or spots

speech (SPEECH) *n.* the act or way of speaking

sport (SPORT) *n.* active play that is done to a set of rules

sprout (SPROWT) *n.* a young, new growth from a plant or seed

stam•i•na (STAM i nah) *n.* the strength to carry on

steal (STEEL) *v.* to take away secretly and without permission

sting•er (STING er) *n.* a sharp, pointed part of an insect or animal

stud•ied (STUD eed) *v.* looked at or into carefully; examined or investigated

sur•face (SUR fis) *n.* the top part of anything

sur•pris•ing (suhr PREYEZ ing) *adj.* shocking or amazing

swift•ly (SWIFT lee) *adv.* in a fast manner; quickly

T t

tai•lor (TAY luhr) *n.* a person who makes or repairs clothing

tale (TAYL) *n.* a story, especially about things that are imagined or made up

team•mates (TEEM mayts) *n.* fellow members of a team

tel•e•vi•sion (TEL e vizh en) *n.* the means of sending images by radio waves or wire to a receiver in another location; of, using, used in, or sent by television

ter•ri•to•ry (TER i TOR ee) *n.* an area of land ruled by a nation or state

there•fore (THER for) *adv.* for this or that reason; as a result

thick (THIK) *adj.* great in width or depth from side to side; not thin

though (THOH) *adv.* in spite of the fact that; although; however

thou•sands (THOU zendz) *n.* more than one thousand

thun•der (THUN der) *n.* noise in an electrical storm caused by moving masses of air

tick•led (TIK uhld) *v.* touched or stroked lightly, as with a finger or feather, so as to cause twitching or laughing

tight•en (TEYET n) *v.* to strain; become taut

ti•ny (TEYE nee) *adj.* very small

trav•el (TRAV uhl) *v.* to go from one place to another

trots (TRAHTS) *v.* steps along quickly

trust•ed (TRUHST ed) *v.* believed in or depended upon as a result of being honest or fair

truth (TROOTH) *n.* what is true, honest, sincere, accurate

twigs (TWIGZ) *n.* small branches of a tree or shrub

U u

un•der•stand (uhn der STAND) *v.* to get the meaning of; know what is meant by something or someone

V v

voic•es (VOYS ez) *n.* sounds of people speaking

vol•ca•no (vol KAY noh) *n.* an opening in the earth's surface through which molten rock is thrown up

W w

wan•der (WAHN der) *v.* to go from place to place in an aimless way; ramble; roam

warn•ings (WORN ingz) *n.* things that tell of danger; advice to be careful

wealth•y (WEL thee) *adj.* having wealth; rich

weath•er (WETH er) *n.* the conditions outside at any time and place with regard to such things as temperature, sunshine, and rainfall

wick•ed (WIK ed) *adj.* bad or harmful on purpose; evil

wid•ow (WID oh) *n.* a woman whose husband has died and who has not married again

wil•der•ness (WIL der nes) *n.* a wild region or wasteland

wreck (REK) *n.* the remains of something that has been destroyed or badly damaged

Answer Key

Bee Bandits Busted
pages 3-7

Getting the Details
a stinger

Alphabet Gets Busy
1. battle
2. carry
3. crowd
4. enter
5. force
6. greedy
7. possible
8. robber
9. several
10. stinger

Words Make Meaning
1. d   3. h   5. a   7. c   9. g
2. j   4. e   6. i   8. f   10. b

Sentences Lose Sting Without Words
1. possible, stinger
2. robber, greedy
3. force, carry
4. enter, crowd
5. Several, battle

Antonyms Are Opposite
1. enter
2. add
3. greedy
4. fat
5. danger
6. teach

Book Writers Bumble, Jumble Words
1. stinger
2. greedy
3. crowd
4. enter
5. several
6. robber
7. force
8. battle
9. possible
10. carry

Test-taking Secrets Revealed
1. B   3. D   5. B   7. C   9. A   11. D
2. A   4. C   6. A   8. D   10. B   12. A

Amazing Plant Comes Back to Life
pages 13-17

Details Take Root in Story
Its roots grow into the ground.

Alphabet Branches Out
1. amazing
2. desert
3. drifts
4. moisture
5. roots
6. scarce
7. search
8. sprout
9. twigs
10. wander

Words Thirst for Meaning
1. i   3. b   5. d   7. g   9. c
2. j   4. f   6. e   8. a   10. h

Sentences Sprout New Words
1. twigs
2. wander
3. roots
4. amazing
5. drifts
6. sprout
7. moisture
8. search
9. scarce
10. desert

Words Have Happy Endings
1. searches, searched, searching
2. carries, carried, carrying
3. hopes, hoped, hoping
4. drips, dripped, dripping

Analogies Are Everywhere
1. desert
2. scarce
3. amazing
4. roots
5. moisture
6. search

Test-day Tips Told
1. C   3. A   5. D   7. B   9. D   11. C
2. B   4. D   6. C   8. C   10. B   12. D

Sewing Is for the Birds!
pages 8-12

Keys to Story Revealed
his bill

Alphabet All Sewed UP
1. female
2. fluffy
3. hatched
4. knots
5. male
6. material
7. pokes
8. prepares
9. sews
10. tailor

Words Hold Nest Egg of Meaning
1. c   3. i   5. e   7. b   9. h
2. j   4. f   6. g   8. d   10. a

Sentence Holes Filled with Words
1. sews
2. material
3. tailor
4. knots
5. pokes
6. fluffy
7. prepares
8. hatched
9. male
10. female

So What Do You Sew?
1. c   a. or
2. b   b. creek
3. a   c. hair
4. b   d. heel
5. c   e. male
6. a

The Word Search Is On

```
F Q K N O T S C M R
E T A I L O R V A H
M A L E Y S W A T L
A M K Z O E P E X
L B E D J W O V R M
E K H I E S K C I D
P R E P A R E S A W
P R Q A D C S Y L T
L N F L U F F Y E C
R D H A T C H E D L
```

Score Higher on Tests
1. C   7. A
2. B   8. D
3. B   9. B
4. C   10. C
5. B   11. B
6. A   12. C

On the Trail of a Kangaroo's Tail
pages 18-22

Story Hopping with Details
a car

Alphabet Keeps Letters in Order
1. automobile
2. balance
3. crutch
4. forward
5. kangaroos
6. leap
7. pouch
8. powerful
9. tale
10. travel

Words and Meanings—Match Them Up
1. d   3. a   5. b   7. j   9. e
2. i   4. h   6. f   8. c   10. g

Suffixes Get Words Hopping
1. powerful
2. joyful
3. thoughtful
4. colorful
5. forgetful
6. careful
7. helpful
8. cheerful

New Words Complete Sentences
1. automobile
2. powerful
3. tale
4. travel
5. kangaroos
6. pouch
7. crutch
8. forward
9. balance
10. leap

Strange Drawings Are Baffling
1. balance
2. travel
3. crutch
4. tale
5. leap
6. automobile
7. kangaroos
8. pouch

Secrets to Success on Tests
1. C   3. A   5. B   7. B   9. A   11. B
2. B   4. D   6. C   8. B   10. A   12. B

108

Look at Those Dogs Go!
pages 23-27

Find the Details in Record Time
Nome

Alphabet Kept in Order
1. courage
2. huskies
3. language
4. mushers
5. racing
6. reins
7. sometimes
8. sport
9. voices
10. wilderness

Match Words and Meanings in a Hurry
1. e 3. h 5. b 7. j 9. d
2. c 4. a 6. g 8. i 10. f

Words Race to Finish Sentences
1. courage
2. wilderness
3. mushers
4. sport
5. Sometimes
6. voices
7. reins
8. language
9. racing
10. huskies

Word Meanings Changed
1. unreal
2. untie
3. unwrap
4. uneaten
5. untie
6. uneaten
7. unreal
8. unwrap

Solve This Puzzle and Win the Race
Across
3. voices
6. language
7. reins
10. huskies

Down
1. racing
2. wilderness
4. sometimes
5. mushers
8. sport
9. courage

Secrets to Success on Tests
1. C 3. A 5. D 7. C 9. C 11. B
2. B 4. C 6. A 8. A 10. D 12. D

Dream World Explained!
pages 28-32

What's the Big Idea?
People have studied dreams and found out many things.

Vocabulary Wishes and Alphabet Dreams
1. adults
2. allowed
3. blind
4. during
5. grouchy
6. hardly
7. recently
8. sound
9. studied
10. though

Discover the Hidden Meaning
1. d 3. i 5. h 7. j 9. g
2. f 4. a 6. e 8. b 10. c

Dream Words Fit Perfectly!
1. studied
2. though
3. adults
4. allowed
5. blind
6. sound
7. hardly
8. grouchy
9. recently
10. during

Suffixes Provide Happy Endings!
1. recently
2. slowly
3. sadly
4. quickly
5. Sadly
6. Recently
7. slowly
8. quickly

Words Riddled with Secret Meaning!
1. sound
2. blind
3. grouchy
4. though
5. studied
6. *dream*
7. adults
8. during
9. recently

Riddle Answer: nightmare

Improve Your Score
1. B 3. A 5. B 7. D 9. C
2. D 4. C 6. B 8. A 10. B
9. C
10. A

"Little House" Lady Lives on in Books
pages 33-37

A Walk Down Main-idea Street
a lady who wrote about her life

Alphabet Helps Tell Stories
1. born
2. cabin
3. interesting
4. mind
5. past
6. prairie
7. settlers
8. space
9. television
10. territory

Words Find Missing Meanings
1. d 3. i 5. a 7. b 9. e
2. c 4. j 6. h 8. f 10. g

Syllables Make Words Grow
1. tel e vi sion
2. prai rie
3. ter ri to ry
4. ad ven ture
5. cab in
6. in ter est ing
7. set tlers
8. au to mo bile
9. ma te ri al
10. en ter tain ment

Missing Words
past
settlers
cabin
prairie
space
television
mind
territory
interesting
born

Mixed-up Words Unscrambled
1. territory
2. settlers
3. born
4. past
5. prairie
6. mind
7. space
8. television
9. cabin
10. interesting

Test-taking Secrets Revealed
1. C 3. C 5. B 7. B 9. D 11. A
2. A 4. C 6. C 8. C 10. D 12. D

Even the Moon Gets Blue
pages 38-42

Main Idea Found Once in a Blue Moon
how an old saying about the moon may have begun

Alphabet Keeps Words in Order
1. amount
2. area
3. atmosphere
4. disasters
5. expect
6. forest
7. globe
8. history
9. huge
10. volcano

Words Take Off in Search for Meaning
1. d 3. g 5. e 7. f 9. h
2. a 4. b 6. j 8. i 10. c

Incomplete Sentences Need Help Now!
1. huge
2. forest
3. volcano
4. history
5. amount
6. area
7. atmosphere
8. globe
9. expect
10. Disasters

Synonyms Seem Similar
1. large
2. giggle
3. quantity
4. dampness
5. tale
6. forest
7. automobile
8. right

Close Study Reveals New Words
```
D V E N T A R E A U
E X P E C T O R Y S
D U S T A M O U N T
I S F A S O T V E R
S M O H I S T O R Y
A O R U N P R L E S
S T E G M H O C S P
T H S E R E C A N O
E O T B E R G N E U
R G L O B E L O C A
S D G T N Y O K U M
```

Score Higher on Tests
1. C 7. D
2. D 8. C
3. A 9. A
4. C 10. D
5. B 11. C
6. C 12. A

109

Who Knows How Scratch-and-Sniff Stickers Are Made?
pages 43-47

Look for the Main Idea
how scratch-and-sniff stickers work and are used

Stick to the Alphabet

actor	magazines	school
advertising	*mainly*	scratch
capsules	modern	*secret*
cardinal	perfumes	surprising
cough	*piece*	tiny
dinner	scent	

Scratchers Are Matchers
1. i   3. b   5. f   7. a   9. j
2. e   4. c   6. g   8. h   10. d

Sniff Out the Missing Words
1. perfumes   6. tiny
2. advertising   7. scent
3. magazines   8. capsules
4. cough   9. modern
5. scratch   10. surprising

Small Words Combine for New Meaning
1. *lifetime*   6. popcorn
2. doghouse   7. snowflake
3. starfish   8. birthday
4. raincoat   9. bluebird
5. paintbrush   10. sunburn

Stick Is to Sticker as Tick Is to Ticker
1. modern   3. tiny   5. magazines
2. autumn   4. lifetime   6. human

Test-day Tips Told
1. C   3. A   5. A   7. B   9. B   11. C
2. D   4. C   6. D   8. D   10. D   12. B

Mysterious Goose Bumps Appear
pages 53-57

Shivering Sequence
1. you feel cold
2. nerves communicate a message to your brain
3. your brain tells your muscles to tighten
4. a muscle contracts

Alphabet Puts Words in Order

bluebird	contract	*interior*	skin
cells	follicle	involuntary	surface
communicate	*football*	shivering	*sweeten*
complain	insulation	*shock*	tighten

Words Match with Meanings
1. i   3. j   5. e   7. h   9. b
2. d   4. g   6. f   8. a   10. c

Words Warm Up Sentences
1. cells   6. communicate
2. involuntary   7. insulation
3. shivering   8. tighten
4. follicle   9. surface
5. skin   10. contract

Homonyms Sure Sound Alike
1. d   5. heard
2. c   6. sail
3. a   7. cells
4. b   8. sale

You Get the Picture!
1. contract   5. involuntary
2. follicle   6. communicate
3. surface   7. shivering
4. skin   8. insulation

Secrets to Success on Tests
1. A
2. B
3. B
4. C
5. A
6. C
7. C
8. B
9. B
10. D
11. C
12. D

Small Wonders Score Big
pages 48-52

Main Idea Slams the Point Home
short basketball players

Alphabet Brings Order to Words

banner	*hammer*	rebounding
basketball	nearly	shooting
blocking	need	*shop*
box	opponents	teammates
court	quick	
guard	*quit*	

Words and Meanings Match Up
1. d   3. j   5. h   7. a   9. f
2. g   4. e   6. b   8. c   10. i

Short and Tall Sentences Completed
1. basketball   6. shooting
2. teammates   7. nearly
3. court   8. guard
4. opponents   9. quick
5. rebounding   10. blocking

Little Prefix Makes Big Difference
1. reorder   3. reheat   5. relock
2. reorganize   4. refigure   6. recount

And the Category Is . . . .
1. ball, players, backboard
2. stores, banks, offices
3. vacations, buildings, meetings
4. dribbling, rebounding, shooting
5. roads, halls, openings

Improve Your Score
1. C   3. C   5. D   7. B   9. B   11. B
2. A   4. B   6. A   8. A   10. D   12. C

Widow Goes on Blind Date
pages 58-62

Story Spins Sequence Web
The black widow's mate dies.

Alphabetically Speaking

attest	common	*house*	shiny
attic	*complain*	mate	*ship*
cattle	dines	*shame*	wicked
cause	hourglass	shape	widow

Meanings Discovered
1. j   3. h   5. c   7. b   9. f
2. i   4. e   6. a   8. g   10. d

Sentence Holes Filled at Last
1. widow, mate
2. hourglass, attic
3. wicked, cause
4. dines, common
5. shiny, shape

Less Means More with Suffixes
1. shapeless   6. harmless
2. colorless   7. flavorless
3. senseless   8. careless
4. fearless   9. useless
5. powerless   10. worthless

No More Cross Words!

Across
1. shape
3. widow
5. cause
6. attic

Across
7. mate
8. dines
9. shiny

Down
2. hourglass
4. wicked
5. common

Secrets to Success on Tests
1. C   3. B   5. D   7. D   9. D   11. B
2. C   4. A   6. B   8. B   10. C   12. A

This Gorilla Can Talk to You
pages 63-67
One Thing Leads to Another
Koko learned to use sign language.
Going Ape for the Alphabet

color	gorilla	speech
combed	messages	*spell*
deaf	*metal*	therefore
dear	normal	tickled
form	*nose*	
fort	pill	

Words Seek Meanings
1. g 3. b 5. f 7. e 9. j
2. i 4. c 6. a 8. d 10. h

Incomplete Sentences Just Don't Add Up
1. deaf 6. form
2. Therefore 7. combed
3. normal 8. tickled
4. pill 9. messages
5. speech 10. gorilla

Multiple Meanings Could Spell Trouble
1. b 3. a
2. a 4. b

Word Search Is Monkey Business

```
M E S S E E C T M H S
N C O M B E D I E O R
A L D E N A F C S G O
R I L F O P L K S A T
H E G O R I L L A R E
F O E R M L S E G C S
O M B M A L A D E G P
S A R T L T D O S R E
M F T H E R E F O R E
T H E R E F A R M A C
L N O R L E F D L L H
```

Test-taking Secrets Revealed
1. A 7. C
2. B 8. D
3. C 9. B
4. A 10. B
5. C 11. D
6. B 12. C

Icebergs Lurk in Ocean
pages 68-72
Sequence Frozen in Story
Thick ice forms on land.
Alphabet Puts Words on Ice

aloud	*icicle*	*thin*
although	melt	warnings
damaged	*member*	weather
dance	received	wreck
frozen	*recipe*	
icebergs	thick	

Words Adrift Without Meaning
1. g 3. e 5. h 7. c 9. d
2. b 4. j 6. i 8. f 10. a

Words Finish Sentences
1. wreck 6. icebergs
2. frozen 7. warnings
3. Although 8. thick
4. melt 9. received
5. weather 10. damaged

Word Endings Are Just the Tip of the Iceberg!
1. easier, easiest 4. lazier, laziest
2. flatter, flattest 5. hotter, hottest
3. whiter, whitest 6. nicer, nicest

Secret Code Reveals New Name for the Titanic
1. ALTHOUGH
2. WARNINGS
3. THICK
4. ICEBERGS
THE UNSINKABLE TITANIC

Score Higher on Tests
1. D 3. A 5. C 7. C 9. B 11. D
2. B 4. D 6. C 8. B 10. A 12. C

Who Is This Man on the Five Dollar Bill?
pages 73-77
Sequence Keeps Story in Order
Abe decided to do what was right.
The Amazing Alphabet

born/cold	decided	*prey/try*
borrowed	honest	steal
business	*hop/prevent*	trusted
coin	mistake	truth
collect/honor	president	

Words and Meanings United
1. g 3. e 5. h 7. a 9. f
2. d 4. i 6. c 8. b 10. j

Mystery Solved!
1. business 6. truth
2. decided 7. steal
3. borrowed 8. trusted
4. coin 9. mistake
5. president 10. honest

The Truth About Prefixes
1. distrust 5. disobey
2. dislike 6. distrust
3. disobey 7. discontinued
4. discontinue 8. dislikes

Word Mix-up Straightened Out
1. president 6. business
2. truth 7. trusted
3. borrowed 8. steal
4. honest 9. coin
5. mistake 10. decided

Test-day Tips Told
1. B 3. B 5. B 7. A 9. B 11. B
2. D 4. D 6. A 8. D 10. C 12. C

Roadrunner Always on the Move
pages 78-82
Careful Reading Helps Determine Cause
It eats things people do not like.
Race Through the Dictionary with Guide Words

click/dive	glides	*nation/swim*
cliffs	gulps	skinny
directions	*gun/nasty*	speckled
ditches	lizard	swiftly
divide/gum	narrow	

Perfect Match Found Between Words and Meanings
1. j 3. d 5. i 7. a 9. h
2. c 4. f 6. g 8. e 10. b

Sentence Holes Are for the Birds
1. skinny 6. ditches
2. speckled 7. glides
3. lizard 8. swiftly
4. gulps 9. directions
5. narrow 10. cliffs

Synonyms and Antonyms Are Opposites
1. huge, small 4. healthy, sick
2. thin, fat 5. alike, different
3. rich, poor 6. swiftly, slowly

Words of a Feather Group Together
1. birds, planes, skaters
2. tail, body, head
3. juice, milk, food
4. eggs, walls, paintings
5. rabbit, cheetah, horse

Improve Your Score
1. C 3. A 5. B 7. C 9. D 11. B
2. D 4. C 6. C 8. B 10. B 12. A

111

Killer Storm Hits!
pages 83-87

Cause Found in High-flying Story
warnings by the NOAA

Alphabet Avoids Disorder
avenge/classic	*fin/husky*
avoid	findings
board	hurricane
clap	*patch/tie*
cull/drain	path
current	stamina
downward	thunder

Match These Words with the Meanings
1. c   3. j   5. a   7. f   9. g
2. e   4. i   6. h   8. b   10. d

Antonyms Are Words That Are Different
1. war   4. freeze
2. alive   5. south
3. wrong   6. under

Words Blow in to Fill Sentence Holes
1. current   6. findings
2. avoid   7. stamina
3. clap   8. board
4. hurricane 9. path
5. downward   10. thunder

Picture That!
1. board   5. thunder
2. hurricane 6. current
3. path   7. findings
4. downward   8. avoid

Secrets to Success on Tests
1. A   3. B   5. A   7. D   9. D   11. B
2. D   4. B   6. C   8. B   10. C 12. B

Back to the Future
pages 88-92

Readers Wonder About Cause
TV does not fit in with their religious principles.

Harness This ABC List
avenge/classic	denim	*pretzel/true*
bonnet	discipline	principles
buggy	*harmful/lighten*	shawl
control/dispose	harness	trots
convenience	lifestyle	

Words and Meanings Match
1. h   3. f   5. b   7. i   9. d
2. e   4. c   6. g   8. j   10. a

Hard-working Words Complete the Job
1. principles   6. denim
2. shawl   7. convenience
3. discipline   8. lifestyle
4. trots   9. harness
5. buggy   10. bonnet

Multiple Meanings Can Spell Trouble
1. b   4. b
2. c   5. a
3. a

Secret Answer Revealed
1. bonnet   5. principles   9. *zipper*
2. shawl   6. harness   10. denim
3. trots   7. lifestyle   11. buggy
4. convenience 8. discipline
BARN RAISING

Secrets to Success on Tests
1. B   3. D   5. C   7. D   9. B   11. C
2. A   4. A   6. B   8. B   10. A 12. D

112

Mind Boggling Movies
pages 93-97

Search for the Answers Still On
They seem to move.

New Words Framed! Guide Words Blamed!
calm/dear	film	special
camera	movement	*spend/undo*
cartoons	*much/speed*	thousands
deal	scenery	understand
death/mow	screen	

Words and Meanings All Match Up
1. e   3. d   5. c   7. j   9. g
2. i   4. f   6. a   8. b   10. h

Completed Sentences Give Big Picture!
1. movement   6. film
2. scenery   7. screen
3. thousands 8. camera
4. understand 9. deal
5. cartoons   10. special

Suffixes Change Meaning
1. understandable
2. washable
3. enjoyable
4. passable
5. usable/useable
6. acceptable

Brainstorm Captured on Film
Answers will vary.

Test-taking Secrets Revealed
1. C   3. A   5. A   7. B   9. A   11. C
2. B   4. B   6. B   8. D   10. B 12. B

Young at Heart
pages 98-102

Search for the Details
She wanted children to read about ordinary children like themselves.

The Amazing Alphabet
champion/explode	foreign	rural
characters	humorous	*shock/weather*
difficulty	*hurry/rust*	similar
experiences	neighborhood	wealthy
express/hump	ordinary	

Words and Meanings—Match Them Up
1. c   3. i   5. f   7. h   9. b
2. e   4. j   6. a   8. g   10. d

Incomplete Sentences Need Your Help
rural   wealthy
neighborhood   characters
difficulty   humorous
similar   ordinary
foreign   experiences

Words Divided Over Syllables
1. or di nar y   6. dif fi cul ty
2. wealth y   7. neigh bor hood
3. ru ral   8. hu mor ous
4. ex per i enc es   9. sim i lar
5. for eign   10. char ac ters

Analogies Are Everywhere
1. characters   4. neighborhood
2. wealthy   5. humorous
3. ordinary   6. rural

Score Higher on Tests
1. D   3. D   5. B   7. C   9. D   11. B
2. B   4. A   6. B   8. A   10. B 12. B